Library of
Davidson College

**Namibia:
Political and
Economic
Prospects**

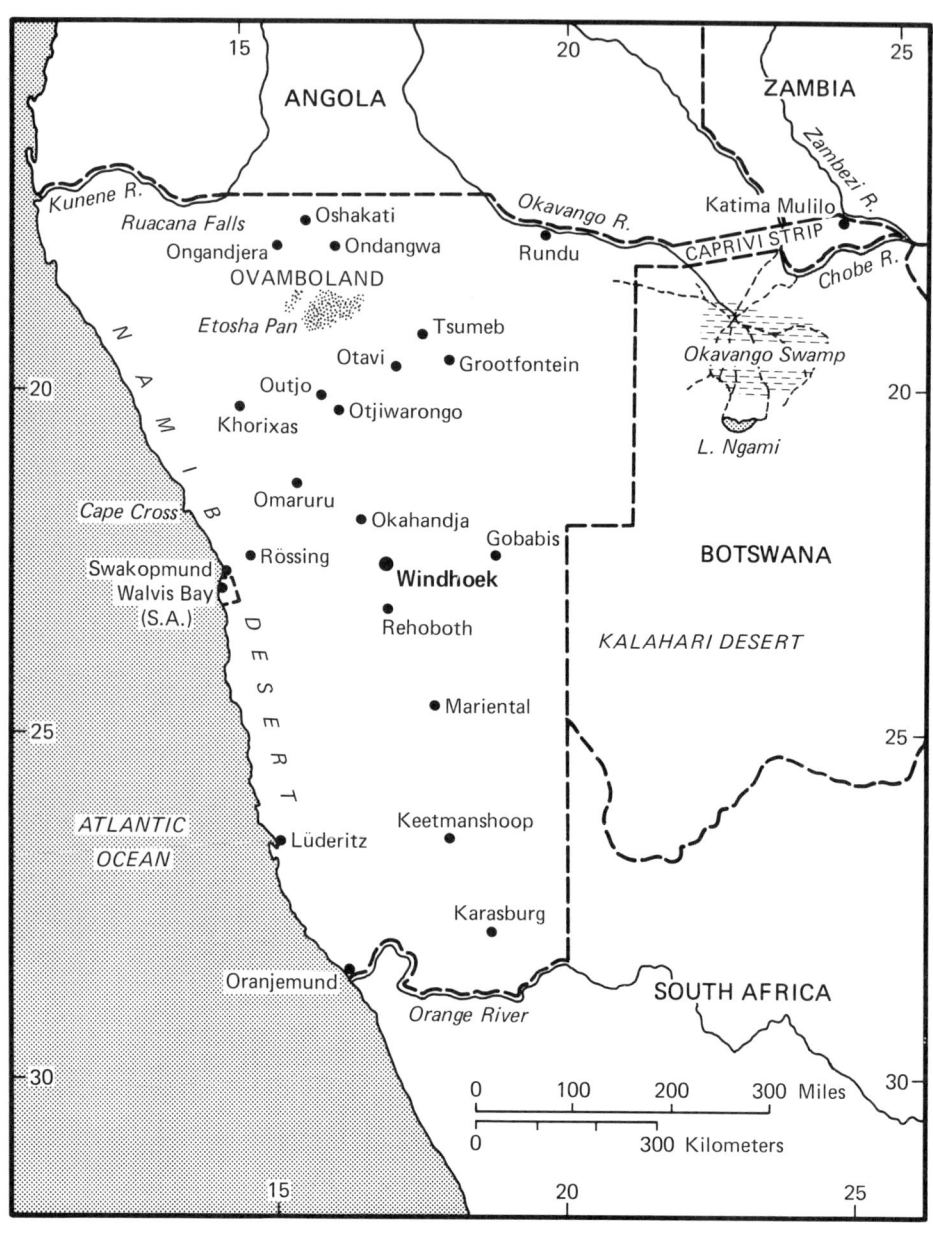

Namibia: Political and Economic Prospects

Edited by
Robert I. Rotberg
Massachusetts Institute of
Technology

LexingtonBooks
D.C. Heath and Company
Lexington, Massachusetts
Toronto

Library of Congress Cataloging in Publication Data
Main entry under title:

Namibia : political and economic prospects.

   Bibliography: p.
   Includes index.
   Contents: The roots of controversy / Nicholas H.Z. Watts—
Political and economic realities in a time of settlement / Robert I.
Rotberg—The economy in transition to independence / Wolfgang H.
Thomas—[etc.]
    1. Namibia—Politics and government—Addresses, essays,
lectures. 2. Namibia—Economic conditions—Addresses, essays,
lectures. I. Rotberg, Robert I.
DT714.N352   1982   320.9688   81–48672
ISBN 0–699–05531–x

Copyright © 1983 by D.C. Heath and Company

All rights reserved. No part of this publication may be reproduced or
transmitted in any form or by any means, electronic or mechanical,
including photocopy, recording, or any information storage or retrieval
system, without permission in writing from the publisher.

Published simultaneously in Canada

Printed in the United States of America

International Standard Book Number: 0–669–05531–x

Library of Congress Catalog Card Number: 81–48672

Contents

	Introduction *Robert I. Rotberg*	vii
Chapter 1	The Roots of Controversy *Nicholas H.Z. Watts*	1
Chapter 2	Political and Economic Realities in a Time of Settlement *Robert I. Rotberg*	29
Chapter 3	The Economy in Transition to Independence *Wolfgang H. Thomas*	41
Chapter 4	Economic Priorities for an Independent Namibia *Kate Jowell*	93
Chapter 5	SWAPO and the Postindependence Era *Stanley Uys*	101
	Bibliography	115
	Index	123
	About the Contributors	133
	About the Editor	135

Introduction
Robert I. Rotberg

The question of Namibia has long bedeviled international relations and threatened world order. Once the German colony of Südwest Afrika, and then the South African-controlled Mandated Territory of South-West Africa, and subsequently a lapsed Mandate virtually absorbed into the body politic of the Republic of South Africa—while simultaneously becoming a divisive issue for the United Nations—Namibia in the late 1970s became a precise problem in search of a compromise solution.

Although Namibia is neither populous nor rich, as the following chapters make clear, resolving the crisis of the territory's transition to independence, and creating a favorable climate for its subsequent development, are crucial to the peaceful evolution of, and the avoidance of East-West conflict in all of southern Africa. With Zimbabwe in its third year of nationhood, for the West and for Africa Namibia is the most salient item on their mutual continental agendas. The long-standing guerrilla war along the borders of Angola and Namibia has stiffened the determination of all sides to limit, if not end, the conflict. Moreover, for the African and Western contending parties, South Africa's occupation of Namibia is illegal and a threat to peace. Since 1977, the West and Africa have thus attempted, with some coordination, to find a formula by which South Africa would leave Namibia and enable a new government of the majority to be selected in accordance with an overall framework approved by the United Nations.

This book is about the era that will follow a settlement—about the postindependence prospects for a new Namibia. But, in order to inform policymakers and others who will want to be concerned with, and influential in, the process of transition, it ignores neither the past nor the uncertain and changeable present.

A chapter by Nicholas H.Z. Watts summarizes the ways in which South-West Africa became a matter of international concern before and after the demise of the League of Nations. When the United Nations came into being, it attempted to bring Namibia under its aegis. But South Africa refused and was taken to court. Watts explains the legal maneuverings and also discusses the origin of articulated African antagonism toward continued South African hegemony. His chapter completes a setting of the scene by reminding readers of South Africa's attempt to bring about an internal settlement and of the more recent twists and turns in the negotiations between the West and South Africa.

My own chapter sets the problems of postindependence Namibia in a contemporary framework. Without examining all of the elements in the 1982 version of the Western-proposed settlement plan, it indicates the nature of the geopolitical and diplomatic decisions that are involved for South Africa, and also for Africa and the West. It debunks the assumptions that are commonly made about Namibia's present and future, and stresses the many ways in which a rapid and easily understood settlement would assist the postindependence maturation of a new Namibia.

The chapter by Wolfgang Thomas provides a comprehensive picture, with a wealth of helpful statistical detail, of the economic structure of the territory. The chapter by Kate Jowell focuses on a number of the priorities for economic development. Together, these two chapters provide as current an exposition as possible of the economic problems of and prospects for Namibia.

Stanley Uys's chapter argues that the main guerrilla group has mixed prescriptions for Namibia, the precise ingredients of each depending to some extent upon the nature of and the way in which the settlement is achieved. Thomas examines a number of the same geopolitical possibilities.

This book stems in part from a conference organized by the World Peace Foundation of Boston, and cosponsored by the Ditchley Foundation of Britain. The conference, held at Ditchley Park, near Oxford, in late 1981, drew thirty-six leading diplomatic, political, economic, and academic participants from Namibia, South Africa, Britain, France, Japan, Canada, and the United States to a meeting that was tightly focused on the postindependence prospects for Namibia. Thomas's chapter was originally prepared for that meeting. Uys was its rapporteur, and his report of the conference is listed in the bibliography. Jowell's chapter emerged from a report originally prepared for a special study group at the conference.

The editor and the contributors are grateful to Alfred O. Hero, Jr. (until recently, executive director of the World Peace Foundation) and to Sir Philip Adams (then the director of the Ditchley Foundation) for their varied, timely, and generous support, their enthusiasm, and their sensitivity in times of crisis. Without their collaboration, and the collaboration of their staffs, the conference could not have succeeded in focusing so precisely on the main issues of an emergent Namibia. John Barratt, the director of the South African Institute of International Affairs, also assisted significantly in the process of making the meeting a success. Andrea Probyn contributed to the smooth organization of the meeting and edited the contributions to this book with her usual consummate skill. Donna L. Rogers collected the material for the bibliography.

1

The Roots of Controversy

Nicholas H.Z. Watts

More than sixty years have passed since the government of South Africa accepted the mandate, and the "sacred trust of civilization" for the people of South-West Africa, from the League of Nations. Until the end of World War II, South Africa's actions, as the mandatory power, attracted little criticism, although they were frequently not in the spirit of the "trust." After the war, the picture of world politics changed rapidly. The British Empire was transformed into a commonwealth of independent sovereign states, and colonial Africa gained its independence not only from Great Britain but from France, Belgium, and, more slowly, from Portugal. Rhodesia tried to stand against this march of history, but it, too, was eventually brought to independence, under black majority rule, in 1980. Yet, throughout this period of change, South-West Africa made little progress toward self-determination and remained under the control of a government in Pretoria that had earned almost universal condemnation for its institutionalization of racist policies.[1]

The history of the territory falls into four distinct phases: the mandate until 1946, the role of the United Nations from 1946 to 1972, the turning of the tide between 1972 and 1977, and the negotiations between South Africa and the Contact Group of Western Nations, which have continued ever since. Until 1972 jurisdiction in international law was the primary issue, but more recently this question has been superseded by the *realpolitik* that attends the arbitration and transfer of power. Joining these issues are the actions of the government of South Africa. The history of the steady defiance by South Africa of first the League of Nations and then the United Nations provides an important prologue to recent political bargaining and to the prospects for an independent and sovereign Namibia.

Underlying this long conflict have been a number of mutually reinforcing suspicions. The indigenous people of South-West Africa soon learned to fear the white settlers, for the German colonists in the late nineteenth century took their land by force and tolerated no dissent. There were several revolts; the harshest repression was meted out to the Herero in 1904 when they were driven from their pastures into the arid Omaheke *sandveld* and were decimated. During World War I, numerous promises were made to the peoples of Namibia concerning the restoration of their lands: the speed with which their expectations were dashed when peace came reinforced their suspicion of whites, whether German, Afrikaner, or British. Afrikaner perceptions had been scarred by the Anglo-Boer War, leaving a bitterness that would find expression forty years later in widespread sympathy for the Nazi cause. Western refusal to permit South Africa to annex the territory fueled this antagonism, and the growing criticism throughout the world of Pretoria's domestic policies increased feelings of rejection and isolation.

The Mandate to 1946

At the end of World War I, the Allies were faced with the question of what to do with the territories that previously had been under the aegis of the defeated nations. The normal rules of conquest at that time, which would have countenanced annexation by the victors, were constrained by two new factors. First was the concept, already taking form in response to the horror of the war, of the League of Nations, which was expected to restrain the behavior of sovereign states through the legal power vested in its Permanent Court of International Justice. The second factor was the sensitivity of President Woodrow Wilson and a newly powerful United States to the concept of self-determination.[2]

The novelty of this position was reflected in the thinking of the principal powers. Much of the early discussion took place before the signing of the Treaty of Versailles in June 1919, when Germany relinquished all of her possessions. In January 1919 the governments of Great Britain and the Union of South Africa agreed that the latter should annex South-West Africa, which it had held since ousting the Germans in 1915. Other allied powers had similar intentions toward territories under their control. Wilson, however, was adamant that he could not return to the United States with the world divided among the Great Powers. Eventually a compromise was accepted in which the disputed territories became mandates, some to be administered as integral portions of the mandatory power. This system owed much to a pamphlet published earlier by Jan Smuts, from which he had deliberately excluded Africa to facilitate the annexation of South-West Africa by South Africa.[3]

Mandates were divded into three categories—Classes A, B, and C—which represented broadly three descending capabilities for self-government. South-West Africa was declared a Class C mandate, and the mandatory power was conferred on the Union of South Africa, on behalf of the British Empire, in May 1919. The League of Nations came into existence in January 1920, and the terms of the mandate were subsequently ratified by the League Council in conformity with Article 22 of the Covenant of the League.

Article 22 is far from explicit about the extent of the power conferred on an administering country. A deliberately ambiguous wording was adopted to satisfy both those parties seeking annexation and those favoring self-determination. There was, however, an explicit understanding that annexations could occur in the future. The article begins by referring to the peoples of former German and Turkish colonies who were "not yet able to stand by themselves under the strenuous conditions of the modern world" and declares that their well-being constitutes "a sacred trust of civilization." It then describes the aim of the mandates as "the tutelage of such people" and defines the different classes of mandate. Some, mainly those previously under Turkish control, could be provisionally recognized as independent nations. For others, the mandatory power was to be responsible for administration but restrictions would be applied that were related primarily to the maintenance of international peace. Finally, some territories, such as South-West Africa, were considered to be best "administered under the laws of the mandatory as integral parts of its territory." The article avoided two central issues: the relationship between white settlers and the indigenous peoples of the mandated territories and the question of where sovereignty for the territory was vested. The intention was to bypass these issues so that the League of Nations could be founded in a spirit of magnanimity and concord; the effect was to generate many years of contention.[4]

The spirit in which South Africa approached the "sacred trust" of the mandate can be seen from examining the three areas that concern most of the correspondence between the administrator for the territory and the Permanent Mandates Commission, which was responsible to the League Council for monitoring the execution of the mandate. The key issues were land allocation and control of Africa labor; further indications of intent were provided by the size of funding for such programs as African education.

If South Africa had chosen a path of racial integration, South-West Africa might have been annexed without international criticism. The South African government had started to introduce legislation to segregate the racial groups within its own borders well before the mandate for South-West Africa was accepted. With the acquisition of the freely worded mandate, the South African government lost little time in transferring similar laws to South-West Africa. In 1920 the Masters and Servants Proclamation was announced which prohibited Africans from leaving white employment under most conditions. In 1922 pass laws were introduced under the Native Administration Proclamation, and Africans working in white areas were required to obey a curfew.

Between 1920 and 1926 more than 1,200 settlers arrived in the territory and were allocated 8.5 million hectares, and as early as 1921 the administrator was justifying the failure to return to the Herero the land taken from them by the Germans on the grounds that vested rights made it impossible. Those rights could only belong to the Germans who remained in the territory or to the 169 settlers who arrived during 1920. At Versailles, it had been decided that Germany should lose its colonies, in part because of the ill treatment it had accorded its colonial peoples, but less than three years later Germans in South-West Africa were being allowed to retain the land that they had taken forcibly from the Herero and other tribes. The action was justified in the name of segregation. The Herero were given a reserve in the same *sandveld* into which they had previously been driven. Overall, some 8.8 million hectares were set aside for tribal reserves, of which 8 million were *sandveld*. The reserve for the Nama (Bondels) allowed 400 acres per family, which was inadequate in view of the poor quality of the land; the average size for white-owned farms was 37,000 acres.

Implicit in the priority given to white settlers over Africans in matters of land allocation was the dependence of the white farmers upon cheap black labor. The most disheartening example of how this labor was obtained can be seen in the account of the Bondelswarts rebellion of 1922. Some Nama (Bondels) had worked as trackers for the South Africans during the fighting against the Germans, but they had not been given back their former lands. They were forced to find a living by hunting game with packs of dogs. Their success limited the number of Nama who found it necessary to seek work on white farms. The Germans moved to assure the supply of black labor by shooting the dogs, but in 1917 the South Africans instituted, instead, a tax which was considered to be a more humane means of achieving the same end. In 1921 the tax was raised and the Nama were unable to pay it even by selling their cattle at low prices. Goaded by this tax and other restrictions, they rebelled. The administrator put himself at the head of a force of armed volunteers and used aircraft to bomb the Nama *laager* (defenses); more than one hundred were killed. The government's actions were censured by the Permanent Mandates Commission, although in muted terms, and this criticism may have prompted the more restrained use of force by which a revolt of the Basters was quelled in 1925.

The Bondelswarts rebellion resulted in an important legal decision concerning the mandate. One of the leaders of the Nama was Jacobus Christian. He was captured and charged in 1924 with treason. Under the Roman law of South Africa, treason is a *crimen laesae majestatis*, requiring the South African government to prove that it had *majestas*, or sovereignty, over the territory. After lengthy reasoning, the South African

Supreme Court ruled that South African sovereignty did extend to South-West Africa.

During the late 1920s the education budget for South-West Africa typically allocated about £11,000 for Africans compared with £120,000 for whites. At the end of the decade almost one hundred government and private schools existed for whites, but fewer than sixty had been provided for the much more numerous blacks. The administrator drew a parallel with figures for South Africa but, as the Permanent Mandates Commission pointed out, there was in one case a responsibility to taxpayers and in the other the obligation of the sacred trust. During the 1930s, the commission continually regretted that it could find no evidence to show that the Africans were being brought closer to self-determination, and in 1935 it recorded that the system of reserves for Africans seemed designed to perpetuate the existing state of affairs since even after fifteen years not one African was educated enough to sit on any native council or on the Advisory Council.

The commission was generally restrained in its criticism, and found much to praise in the work of the South African administration. Two arguments can be made in defense of this seemingly weak response. First, the League was very Eurocentric and not very concerned with southern Africa. In addition, Smuts was a respected world statesman and a principal architect of the League. Second, the League was more concerned with preserving relations between English- and German-speaking whites in the territory than with the treatment of Africans.

The United Nations Seeks a Solution, 1946–1972

The League of Nations was dissolved in 1946. All of the other mandated territories it had created were either given independence or turned into trusts in accordance with Chapter XII of the new United Nations charter. The government of South Africa, however, refused to accept the trusteeship proposal for South-West Africa. It refused to recognize that the United Nations had any authority in the issue. Pretoria argued that the mandate had lapsed and that South Africa therefore had the right to annex the territory. South African advocates repeatedly ignored the fact that the territory was one of several classes of mandate and that the declared objective of that mandate, self-determination for the people of the territory, was incompatible with integration into another state. South Africa acceded to strong opposition in the United Nations and stopped short of formal annexation; it preferred instead to govern as it had done in the prewar years, under all of the conditions of annexation except formal legislation.

The United Nations sought to bring South-West Africa under the trusteeship system by means of resolutions in the General Assembly and through the work of a series of committees. From 1951 to 1953 an ad hoc committee of the General Assembly tried unsuccessfully to reach agreement with South Africa. The talks foundered on two issues. First was a fundamental disagreement over how South Africa's administration of the territory should be supervised. The second stumbling block was the question of recognition of the authority of the United Nations in this matter; Pretoria had refused since 1949 to provide the United Nations with the annual reports that it had furnished previously under the terms of the mandate. Instead, South Africa wished to make a new agreement with three of the principal powers who had created the mandate: the United Kingdom, France, and the United States.

In 1953, after the ad hoc committee had admitted failure, the General Assembly set up another committee on South-West Africa to attempt to carry out the supervisory functions previously exercised by the League. South Africa failed to recognize the committee and refused to cooperate with it. In 1956 the General Assembly sought the direct intervention of the Secretary-General but this, too, failed to achieve anything. In 1957 the Good Offices Committee was established by the General Assembly. It comprised the United Kingdom and the United States, with Brazil selected as the third member by the secretary-general. It met with South African officials, but its own proposals for a solution, based upon either a modified mandate or on the trusteeship system, were rejected by South Africa—which made a counterproposal for partition, with the southern part of the territory to be annexed by South Africa. This suggestion was forcefully rejected by the assembly, and in 1959 the committee reported that it, too, had failed to find a formula for resolving the issue.

Meanwhile, in 1949, the General Assembly had sought a ruling from the International Court of Justice at The Hague on the status of South-West Africa. The opinion of the court, delivered in 1950, was that, if the mandate had lapsed as South Africa claimed, then South African authority over the territory would also have lapsed; since it still exercised de facto authority, the mandate was still in force and somebody must assume the responsibilities previously vested in the League. This body could only be an organ of the United Nations and was in effect the General Assembly. This decision by the court explicitly established the assembly as the successor to the League. The court further ruled that South Africa had no power to change the status of the territory unilaterally. Implicit was the assumption that the assembly did have authority to change that status, and this assumption is the legal foundation upon which the case has been based for the role of the assembly in determining the statehood of South-West Africa.

The court heard two other cases, in 1955 and 1956, on minor issues concerning South-West Africa. In each case, South Africa appeared before the court, but the cause of self-determination was poorly served. The rulings were binding on the General Assembly, as an organ of the United Nations, but were not binding on South Africa, as an individual state. That discrepancy raised the unresolved question of whether (since the mandate made the General Assembly and South Africa partners to a form of treaty) an opinion that was binding on one party should be binding on the other. By the end of the 1950s, the nations of black Africa realized that, in their fight for South-West African independence, and for the general overthrow of white minority regimes in southern Africa, they would be helped more if South Africa were brought before the court in a contentious case where the decision would be binding on all parties. Accordingly, a case was brought in 1960. The plaintiffs were Ethiopia and Liberia, which had both been sovereign states in the League of Nations and could thus trace their interest in the mandated territory back to its inception.

The two threads of the dispute, legal and political, came together in this case. South Africa contended that the whole issue was *sub judice* and should be held in abeyance until the court announced its opinion. The assembly rejected this assertion and proceeded to pass resolutions that both addressed and prejudged the issue. Four resolutions charged South Africa with failing to carry out its obligations as a mandatory power before the court finally ruled on the case in 1966.

Far from showing restraint as a result of the case in progress, the wording of resolutions passed by the assembly became stronger in response to pressure from the African states. In 1961, the assembly requested that the United Nations Committee on South-West Africa visit the territory with or without the cooperation of the South African government. The latter informed the secretary-general that any attempt to visit would be thwarted. Instead, the committee visited other African countries and heard petitions from the South-West Africa People's Organization (SWAPO) and from the South-West African National Union (SWANU). The committee reported that the General Assembly should seek to terminate the mandate and assume either direct or indirect administrative control over the territory. South Africa predictably rejected this report.

Following its failure, the committee was transformed into a Special Committee of seven members of the General Assembly. By now emphasis had shifted from seeking to establish a trusteeship to a demand for independence. This hardening of attitudes was undermined in 1962 by the meek wording of a communiqué that followed a visit to the territory by the chairman and vice chairman of the special committee. Their subsequent repudiation of the text did little to repair the damage done to the United Nation's interests. Later in 1962 the special committee was in turn dissolved and its duties assigned to the Special Committee on the Situation with Regard to the Implementation of the Declaration on the Granting of Independence to Colonial Countries and Peoples (the Special Committee of 24).

The Homelands Policy

In 1964 South Africa gave close attention to the matter of extending the apparatus of apartheid to South-West Africa. The basis for this decision was the report of a commission chaired by François Odendaal, which was published that year. The commission was appointed to define the geographical, economic, and political aspects of apartheid in South-West Africa. It recommended ten homelands, of which eight were to be for Africans. The allocation of land was to be 39.6 percent for blacks and 44.1 percent for whites. To implement this policy, over 28 percent of the Africans would have to be relocated. The report was condemned by the United Nations, but the South Africans announced that although they accepted the report they would not implement its recommendations until the International Court had given its opinion.

The first homeland, Ovamboland, was created in 1967. It exercised limited authority over education, justice, finance, and community affairs, but all of its decisions had to be approved by Pretoria. Okavangoland and East Caprivi soon followed, in 1970 and 1972, respectively. Legislative councils of tribal representatives were appointed for both of these homelands by the South African government. In 1971, the establishment of Damaraland was proposed. It was to have an advisory council of prominent Damara chiefs, but the prospective members of this council opposed plans for the establishment of a legislative council similar to those in other homelands, and, therefore, the proposal for limited self-government was formally rejected by the chiefs in 1973.

Some other groups in Namibia had already enjoyed a limited measure of autonomy. The Basters of Rehoboth had established an advisory council in 1928, and the Coloureds had had one since 1961. The Basters maintained a strong tradition of separatism, and in 1975 their council split when five of the seven members supported SWAPO. This tradition had earlier led the council to refuse supervision by South Africa's Ministry of Coloured Affairs; in 1973 a separate Ministry of Rehoboth Affairs was established.

The South African government pressed on with its policy of establishing ethnic homelands, and Kaokoland was created in 1975. The policy did not proceed smoothly, however. The Herero rejected plans for a homeland, but a more significant gesture was the response of the Ovambo electorate in 1973. SWAPO and the Democratic Cooperative Party of Ovamboland (DEMCOP) proclaimed a boycott when the South African government refused to let them take part in the election. It was spectacularly successful: only 2.5 percent of the 42,000 eligible Ovambo voted. The following year, Ovamboland was granted a new constitution, which led to further elections in 1975. This time SWAPO was allowed to participate, but its leaders urged another boycott because of repressive emergency regulations that were still in force. There was only a 55-percent turnout, despite threats that absence of a voting mark on work permits would hamper or disqualify individuals from getting jobs outside the homeland. In August 1975 the chief minister of Ovamboland, Chief Filemon Elifas, who had become increasingly autocratic and had espoused the cause of a separate Ovamboland based on the union of the homeland with the Ovambos of southern Angola, was murdered.

The Deliberations of the International Court, 1960–1966

The judgment at The Hague for which South Africa had waited with such an appearance of propriety was the most contentious ever handed down by the court. It first considered whether the court was qualified to hear the case and whether the applicants had the right to bring it. By a narrow margin of eight votes to seven (the deciding vote being cast by the president of the court), it ruled in 1962 that it was satisfied with both the jurisdiction of the court and the standing of the applicants. In 1966, however, after hearing extensive evidence on the merits of the case, it reversed its decision concerning the applicants' standing (again on the deciding vote of the president) so that the merits of the case were never adjudged.

Ethiopia and Liberia sought the ruling of the court on whether the mandate was a "Treaty in Force" by the terms of Article 37 of the Statutes of the International Court; whether South Africa remained bound by the terms of Article 22 of the mandate; whether, by the practice of apartheid, South Africa had failed to promote the well-being of the inhabitants of the territory under the terms of Article 22; and a number of other lesser matters. The applicants based their case on Article 7.2 of the mandate, which stated that "if any dispute whatever should arise between the mandatory and another member of the League of Nations relating to the interpretation or application of the provisions of the Mandate, such dispute . . . shall be submitted to the Permanent Court of International Justice."[5]

South Africa had raised four preliminary objections and the jurisdictional issues that these questions raised were addressed first by the court. The third objection was that no dispute existed to judge since no material interests of either applicant were affected. In 1966 the court, which was expected to judge the merits of the case, instead reviewed the four objections and found this third argument compelling, putting forward the same line of reasoning that had been presented in dissenting opinions in the 1962 judgment. The court ruled that the mandate was created on behalf of the League of Nations as a collective body and individual states did not derive the right to question a mandatory power about its execution of the mandate simply by virtue of membership in the League. Nations with general objections could bring their complaints to the attention of the League Council. The import of Article 7.2, and the phrase concerning "any dispute whatever," referred to matters of direct concern to an applicant, such as the treatment of missionaries in a mandated territory.

The court that presented its findings in 1966 differed from the court that had sat in 1962. One judge had withdrawn on instructions from the president of the court, although the necessary public meeting was not held to consider his withdrawal. During the trial one judge died and another was too ill to participate; both had voted against South Africa in 1962. Thus, the court was reduced to twelve permanent judges and two ad hoc judges, and the change favored South Africa.

The controversy caused by this judgment focused not on the legal decision, which had been accepted in 1962 as a respectable dissenting opinion, but on the apparent reversal on the question of standing. The main issue in 1962 had been the right of the applicants to bring the case and that right had been accepted. But, in 1966, the court said that the standing of the applicants had only been accepted in principle, and that a consideration of the merits of the case was necessary to determine their true standing. It is a general legal principle that if issues of jurisdiction are judged before the merits of a case are examined, as happened in 1962, one cannot later reverse the process and return to questions of jurisdiction unless the initial decision specified that part of the ruling was being reserved for later examination. Although nowhere explicitly stated, this concept is the foundation of judicial stability and consistency. A parallel can be found in the principle that a person cannot be tried twice for the same offense.

The 1966 decision of the court caused a furor both in legal circles and in the United Nations. It is not clear why the court came to this conclusion, although the wide range of opinions expressed can be explained by the diverse nationalities of the judges and by the differing

The Roots of Controversy

legal schools that they represented. Over time, the applicants had changed the whole thrust of their case to minimize unacceptably heavy legal costs. They focused on the existence of apartheid, rather than on its implementation, as a breach of the mandate. Had the court found in favor of the applicants, the ruling might have been used within the United Nations to support a call for economic sanctions against South Africa in response to apartheid practices within her own borders. Since these sanctions would certainly have been vetoed, the court may have believed that it would undermine its own credibility if it handed down a judgment that would lead to an unenforceable demand for action. Whatever the motives of the court (which may have been purely juridical) the opinion was so widely condemned that it is often considered to be a major factor in the decline of the court's credibility.[6]

The decision destroyed the impetus for action within the United Nations, which had been confident that the court would find against South Africa in an enforceable judgment. The United Nations therefore sought to apply political pressure to achieve its will in South-West Africa by using narrow interpretations of earlier legal judgments. In the meantime, South African propagandists lost no time in claiming the court's decision as a complete vindication of their case.

Although this decision led SWAPO to the conclusion that the only practicable course to freedom was through armed struggle, the General Assembly resolved to revoke the mandate and to take the responsibility for the territory upon itself. The legality of this decision was questionable on three counts. The fundamental objection was that, however the General Assembly maneuvered, it could not prove that South Africa had acted against the rules of international law in its administration of the mandate, although it may have acted against the wishes of the majority of the assembly. There had been no judicial finding against South Africa on this issue; the ruling of 1950 carried with it dissenting opinions that served to support South Africa's position and to diminish the persuasive weight of what was, in any case, only an advisory opinion. In addition, it was necesary to declare South-West Africa to be a territory with international status under Article 2.7 of the United Nations charter, which prohibits intervention by the United Nations in the domestic affairs of any member. Since it was a mandated territory and not a state, some deft phrasing was necessary, and the territory became "the Namibian entity."

The basis upon which the General Assembly arrogated the right to administer the territory is also questionable. The charter does not allow for direct administration of a territory by the General Assembly, but it was impracticable to transfer the responsibility to another state (which would have led the new party either into war with South Africa or into nonfulfillment of its obligations). Therefore, the assembly decided to become the trustee itself. Although it required a resolution in the Security Council to give this decision binding force, the assembly followed through on its policy. In 1967 it decided to establish a United Nations Council for South-West Africa to administer the territory until independence, and to appoint a commissioner to be based in the territory and to act as a liaison with the government in Pretoria. Not surprisingly, the council reported later that year that South Africa had prevented it from complying with the terms of the resolution.

The next step in this political waltz, which was increasingly divorcing itself from reality, was in 1968 to rename the territory "Namibia." South Africa continued to call it South-West Africa.

The Security Council responded to pressure from the General Assembly and called on the South African government to withdraw immediately. Pretoria once again declined, arguing that the assembly was not empowered to terminate the mandate and that any subsequent pronouncements were irrelevant. The Security Council moved slowly through a series of increasingly severe resolutions that carefully eschewed any enforcement action. In 1969 it recognized the legitimacy of the struggle of the people of Namibia against the illegal presence of the South African authorities and urged members to refrain from dealings with Pretoria in matters relating to Namibia. The following year it declared that all acts by the government of South Africa concerning Namibia after the revocation of the mandate were illegal and invalid. Then, in 1970, it asked the International Court to advise member states on the implications of South Africa's defiance of the council and its continued presence in Namibia.

Once again the court first considered preliminary objections by South Africa and held that, since the 1966 judgment had not dismissed the applicants' claim that there was a dispute, a dispute still existed. It lay between South Africa and the whole body of the United Nations rather than any individual member. The court then turned to the revocation of the mandate. It focused on a very narrow point of law relating to the breach of a treaty leading to its termination (which was of limited usefulness since there were no other mandates to which the principle could be applied). Much more significant was the dictum that the court could not dispute the rulings of another body of the United Nations, since this point implied that the General Assembly could determine its own powers wherever these powers were not defined in the charter. The court found that South Africa's presence in Namibia was illegal and that it was incumbent upon member states to support any action taken by the United Nations.

The court gave its opinion in June 1971, and the Security Council agreed with its findings four months later. The ruling against South Africa was generally acceptable outside the legal community. Within that community, however, it was widely held that the court's judgment had been unduly swayed by humanitarian sentiment. Two arguments were put forward against the right of the assembly to revoke the mandate. The first was that South Africa's failure to submit annual reports to the United Nations did not constitute a fundamental breach of treaty as they had only been asked for in response to the advisory opinion of the court in 1950. The second argument was that, although South African administration might have been detrimental to "the material and moral well-being and social progress" of the inhabitants of South-West Africa, this issue had not been subject to a judicial ruling at the time when the General Assembly revoked the mandate.

These cases before the International Court raised important issues. They highlighted the fact that matters of law were becoming subordinated to political interests. This fact is seen most clearly in the action taken by the General Assembly in passing resolutions while the case was *sub judice*, in revoking the mandate, and in giving Namibia international legal status without clear authority. The position of the court was compromised by the circumstances of Judge Mohammad Zafiulla Khan's withdrawal and the reconsideration in 1966 of an issue of standing that had already been decided in the earlier hearing. Throughout this period South Africa's conduct was as correct in regard to the letter of the law as it was removed from the spirit of the mandate. Whatever interpretation is put on these cases, they revealed that the court, working in a relatively new field of law, embodied such wide differences of legal interpretation that its judgments, especially when handed down by narrow margins, did not carry conviction with world leaders.

The Tide Begins to Turn: 1972–1976

The decision by the International Court of Justice, and its acceptance by the Security Council, marked the end of a phase that lasted for more than a decade and was characterized by controversial legal opinions tending to follow in the wake of increasingly militant resolutions by the General Assembly. This militancy reflected the growing awareness in that body of its own impotence. With the decision of the court in 1971, the complex interaction of resolutions and legal findings had gone as far as it logically could: there was little else the court could do to increase the legitimacy of the assembly's actions beyond that already accorded to it by the 1950, 1962, and 1971 judgments.

South Africa rejected the legality of the United Nation's involvement in the issue, and the world body found itself unable to manifest its concern because calls for sanctions of any significant nature were vetoed in the Security Council. In the meantime, the tide was running fast toward independence in the two Portuguese colonies of Angola and Mozambique. Three factors swept this tide across the borders of Namibia. The United Nations was unable to do anything constructive, other than to give its support to SWAPO; growing unrest developed with Namibia, which drew strength from the victories against the Portuguese; and South Africa took a number of measures to increase its control over the territory.

Resentment within Namibia after the ruling of the court found expression in December 1971 when a strike over labor conditions spread among the Ovambo who worked outside the homeland. Workers were bound to employers by contract and it was a criminal offense to change employment. At the end of the contracted period—usually a year or eighteen months—the worker had to return to the homeland before seeking further employment. As a result of the strike, some 13,000 Ovambo were sent back to their homeland. The strike closed down the Tsumeb mining complex and caused considerable disruption of the railways and the fishing industry. The South African authorities made slight changes in the conditions of employment but, by February 1972, they remained sufficiently alarmed at the continuing unrest to introduce what was in effect a state of emergency in the north of Namibia. At the same time South Africa deployed troops in the area, and by the end of the year the powers of the South African police were increased. Measures were announced in March to introduce a system of registration at labor bureaus.

The United Nations was still searching for the formula that would give substance to its numerous resolutions, and in February 1972 the Security Council requested Kurt Waldheim, the secretary-general, to contact all parties concerned, with the aim of enabling the people of Namibia to exercise their right to self-determination and independence. While those contacts were being established, however, South Africa announced that it would create an Advisory Council for Namibia under the prime minister's chairmanship. It was to consist of one representative from the Tswana and the Bushmen and two from each of the other ethnic groups, including the white community. At the first meeting in Windhoek in 1972 there were sixteen representatives; two whites, two Coloureds, and two each from Ovamboland, Kavango, and East Caprivi, with a single representative from the Basters, Bushmen, Damara, Herero, Nama, and Tswana. The same limited representation characterized the second meeting, in Pretoria. In Windhoek, riots expressed popular opposition to the council.

In 1974, the Caetano government in Portugal fell. South Africa found both its flanks exposed because President Samora Machel led the Front for the Liberation of Mozambique (FRELIMO) into power in Mozambique, and, in Angola, the MPLA won a triangular battle for supremacy with support from Moscow and with aid of substantial numbers of Cuban troops. Although the rule of the Popular Movement for the Liberation of Angola (MPLA) and of Agostinho Neto, the new president of Angola, was uncertain, and the forces of Union for the Total Independence of Angola (UNITA) in the south managed to exercise considerable control, there was great concern in Pretoria at this erosion of the "colonial buffer zone" that South Africa had relied upon as part of her defensive strategy. Not only had the borders of black Africa suddenly come much closer but these developments seemed to point toward South Africa's main strategic nightmare: the incorporation of southern Africa into the Soviet camp.

These fears led to an invasion of Angola by South Africa in 1975. The South African troops were initially very successful and pushed north until they were close to Luanda. They then stopped, without achieving any significant military goals. They did not crush the MPLA, they did not capture the capital, and they did not hold important strategic ground. The reason for this sudden loss of nerve seems to have been the unified opposition of world opinion. Whereas the Western nations often opposed black Africa in the United Nations, they stood firm on this issue, and the West made it clear that they would not support military adventurism to overthrow the MPLA goverment. South African leaders had expected to enjoy some international support for their campaign; initially they had received such support, albeit covertly, from the United States and from Zambia. However, they found that the invasion eventually led to a greater measure of isolation from the international community.

South Africa's political losses were sixfold. It failed to regain a buffer state between its border and black Africa; intervention only ensured that Cuban troops would remain in Angola. The invasion had failed to gain Pretoria any time either for internal reform or for a negotiated settlement of the Namibian dispute. International support for SWAPO increased and, at the same time, the South African position at the United Nations was further weakened by the use of Namibia as a base for military operations. The attack jeopardized the few links that Pretoria had with the rest of southern Africa without bringing any commensurate advantages. By 1977, only the Ivory Coast, Zaire, and Malawi maintained diplomatic relations with Pretoria. Prime Minister B. Johannes Vorster had tried to build closer relations with black Africa, believing that these links, and a de facto acceptance of his policies by black leaders, would blunt Western criticism.

The invasion was a brutal response to the demands of the Security Council, which had set a deadline of May 1975 for the withdrawal of South Africa from Namibia. When that deadline passed, the Security Council met to consider further action, but the call for an embargo on all arms sales, put forward by the African bloc, was killed by the vetoes of France, Great Britain, and the United States. By October 1977, however, the Security Council was prepared to unite and impose a compulsory arms embargo under Chapter VII of the United Nations charter, although the same three countries used their vetoes to prevent the implementation of full economic sanctions.

SWAPO also suffered as a result of the invasion, but its costs were military rather than political. SWAPO forces were caught between South African troops and the soldiers of UNITA, with whom SWAPO had previously maintained friendly relations. Jonas Savimbi, UNITA's leader, had supported requests from both Zaire and Zambia for South African intervention to defeat the MPLA.

South Africa responded to its setbacks with characteristic vigor. The number of troops in Namibia was rapidly increased; during 1977 approximately 47,000 were mobilized. Even allowing for some rotation of troops, this was a very large figure and placed a disproportionate burden on the small white population, for whom the opportunity costs of national service were high.

South Africa took other measures, too. Kavango and Caprivi became subject to emergency legislation in 1976. There was a large-scale evacuation of civilians from the border region near Angola; about 20,000 were relocated. Since Ovamboland is the most densely populated part of the country, these measures brought about 55 percent of the population under the restrictive legislation. In addition, mass arrests became frequent and, according to information from Amnesty International, the security forces routinely used torture to extract so-called confessions and information from prisoners and further to intimidate the local population. In June 1976, one thousand men were arrested by a single battalion of South African troops in a security sweep in Ovamboland.

The South African government also took political steps in 1975 in an attempt to reduce international criticism of its actions in Namibia. It called a constitutional conference to decide the future status of the territory. It was convened in September and was called the Turnhalle Conference after the building in Windhoek where it met. Although the conference represented the various ethnic groups of the country, the Legislative Assembly did not allow any nonwhite political parties to attend. The black representatives were drawn from the homeland governments (in the case of the Ovambo, Kavango, Rehoboth Basters, and East Caprivians), from the unelected headmen of the Herero, and from a splinter group of the Damara, which was formed when the Damara Advisory Council refused to take part in the conference. The South African government directly selected the representatives from groups, such as the San (Bushmen), who had no homeland administration. On these

The Roots of Controversy

grounds, as well as on the underlying legal premise that South African authority to take such action had lapsed with the revocation of the mandate, the Turnhalle Conference was criticized by both the United Nations and by the political parties excluded from the talks.

The conference issued an initial declaration of intent followed by an outline of the points upon which there had been agreement. This statement, issued in August 1976, said that the conference had set 31 December 1978 as the date that could "with reasonable certainty" be set for the territory's independence. In March 1977 the conference concluded its work. It petitioned the South African government to establish an interim administration and to approve a constitution for the transitional period.

The draft constitution described the area over which the interim government would have authority as that known as the Mandated Territory of South-West Africa. In so doing, it accepted the South African contention that the Walvis Bay enclave belonged to South Africa. This enclave comprises a good deep-water port and the surrounding countryside: a total of 969 square kilometers. About 10,000 whites live there, and approximately 15,000 blacks, who are contract laborers.

Walvis Bay came under British rule in 1878 and was administered loosely by the Cape Colony. The Cape administration was interested in the area for commercial reasons: ostrich feathers, ivory, and Herero-owned cattle (when the Herero were at peace) were sent to Cape Town. The British were also anxious to limit expansion into the region by Afrikaners. Walvis Bay was formally incorporated into the Cape Colony in 1884.

The Cape Colony also acquired twelve offshore islands, called the Penguin group, which were rich in guano. British sovereignty over these islands was proclaimed in May 1886, and the following February the Cape Colony was authorized to annex all twelve islands. In subsequent negotiations with Germany over the sovereignty of the territory, Great Britain retained control of the islands, as well as of Walvis Bay, on behalf of the Cape Colony. The Germans first arrived in the area in 1884, moving into the hinterland after Adolph Lüderitz, a young trader, established a trading post at the port that now bears his name, some three-hundred miles south of Walvis Bay.

In 1910, Walvis Bay was included in the Cape Province upon the formation of the Union of South Africa. After the Germans were driven from the hinterland in 1915, plans for the mandate were drawn up and, from 1922, Walvis Bay was administered as though it were part of South-West Africa.

Although logic might suggest that the enclave should be incorporated in an independent Namibia, as its only significant port, its legal status as a coastal enclave belonging to South Africa is sound. Loose analogies may be seen in the colonial status of Macao and Hong Kong on the coast of the People's Republic of China. South Africa therefore sees the transfer of the enclave to Namibia as an issue for negotiations between independent states. SWAPO, in contrast, has consistently urged that it should be incorporated into Namibia upon independence on the grounds that it is essential to the Namibian economy and was from 1922 to 1979 administered as a part of Namibia.

The constitution proposed by the Turnhalle Conference called for a three-tier structure of government. There was to be a central administration, a second tier of representative authorities, and a third tier of local authorities. The central government would consist of a Ministers' Council and a president appointed by South Africa who would be largely symbolic. Real power would be exercised by the chairman of the council. Each ethnic group would have one minister, except for the Ovambo who would have two. The legislative authority, known as the National Assembly, was to consist of sixty seats allocated among ethnic groups with four seats per group, the remainder being distributed on a pro-rata basis. An allocation based on 1970 census figures would have been as follows:

Ovambos	12	Kavangos	5	Bushmen	4
Whites	6	Coloureds	5	Basters	4
Damaras	5	Namas	5	Tswanas	4
Hereros	5	East Caprivians	5		

South Africa would maintain control over certain key functions of government including foreign policy, defense, transport, finance, and internal security. At the other end of the spectrum of power, some areas of welfare would be delegated to the second-tier authorities. These areas included almost all education, social welfare, housing, pensions, local security, and general law administration. The allocation of power and the emphasis placed on ethnic segregation, which had been derived from the Odendaal report, made this proposed constitution unacceptable to the international community. Consequently, it offered little hope as a means to end the war against SWAPO or to ease the pressure of world opinion upon South Africa.

Negotiations with the Western Contact Group

South African strategy for handling the increasingly unstable Namibian issue consisted of two elements during 1976: greatly increased military activity and the slowly moving negotiations of the Turnhalle Conference.

The Roots of Controversy

There was hope that the conference would lead to a constitution that would enable an independent Namibia, with a government favorable to Pretoria, to be recognized by the international community.

From 1977, President Jimmy Carter's administration brought to U.S. foreign policy a strong commitment to human rights. His administration and the Western members of the Security Council realized that the traditional paths of United Nations's diplomacy—resolutions by the General Assembly, binding resolutions by the Security Council frequently vetoed by permanent members, and appeals to the International Court of Justice—had converged in a political cul-de-sac. At the same time, instability in southern Africa was bringing urgency to the problem; this was no time for another six-year legal deliberation. Accordingly, Canada, France, Great Britain, the United States, and West Germany decided to act bilaterally with the South African government, the front-line states, and SWAPO. These countries comprised the Contact Group. It was not a formal United Nations's body, but it enjoyed the full support of the organization since it based negotiations upon the formula laid out in the unanimous Security Council Resolution 385 of 1976, which had called for national elections under United Nations's supervision and had "urged all concerned to exert their best efforts towards the achievement of independence by Namibia at the earliest possible date." The Contact Group had the support of the front-line states and of Nigeria who, with the diplomatic leverage of its oil wealth, was playing an increasingly large role in the battle waged by black Africa against apartheid. SWAPO was skeptical of the motives of the Western nations, suspecting that negotiations would only buy time for Pretoria.[7]

The Contact Group made its first visit to South Africa and Namibia in April 1977. During the course of that year, the framework for a possible solution emerged but, concurrent with these efforts, South Africa pursued its own policies for the territory. The interaction of the two processes was at times confusing, and the tone of South Africa's correspondence with the United Nations often seems Orwellian in its disjunction between words and meaning. These communications usually were characterized by South Africa's unflagging adherence to the detail of documents that were either put forward only for planning purposes or were superseded during the course of the diplomatic negotiations. During five years of such negotiations, South Africa never offered a concession in order to move the talks forward. Every concession (some of which were substantial), came in response to the sustained pressure from the other negotiators.

In 1977, in an important change of policy, Vorster announced that the interim government proposed by the Turnhalle convention would not be set up, and he would continue to negotiate with the Contact Group. This reversal was modified by his support for the principles of the Turnhalle formula and by his decision to appoint Judge T. Marthinus Steyn as administrator-general. He also proclaimed the formal annexation of Walvis Bay and the islands by South Africa.

Steyn was allowed remarkable autonomy. He was subject to the South African government but otherwise had power to amend or repeal existing legislation. He also assumed responsibility for most areas that since 1969 had been controlled by ministries in Pretoria, except for defense, foreign affairs, and the police force. He moved rapidly to ease the constraints of apartheid. The Immorality and Mixed Marriages Acts were repealed, the pass laws abolished, and the restrictions on the movement of labor were greatly eased.

SWAPO opposed Steyn's appointment but continued to negotiate with the Contact Group. The pattern that would characterize the talks for the next five years was taking shape as the Contact Group, led by the United States, put pressure on South Africa, while the presidents of the front-line states tried to keep SWAPO amenable to a settlement.

Meanwhile, a historic split occurred in the South-West Africa National Party. Following an unsuccessful bid for the leadership, Dirk Mudge formed the all-white Republican party, pledged to bring Namibia to independence on a multiracial basis. In November 1977, he formed the Democratic Turnhalle Alliance (DTA) with ten parties from the Turnhalle conference.

The Contact Group's final proposal was set out on 10 April 1978. Walvis Bay was excluded, with a note saying that it was a subject for negotiation between South Africa and a sovereign Namibia. The key elements were as follows. A Special Representative from the United Nations was to be appointed. A United Nations Transition Assistance Group (UNTAG) would be created, which would comprise about 5,000 troops and 1,500 civilians. UNTAG would monitor both the cease-fire and the reduction of South African troops over a twelve-week period from the start of that cease-fire. The South African troops would regroup (at Grootfontein and Oshivello, both in the north) and be reduced to 1,500 men. SWAPO forces would regroup at their bases in Angola. Elections would be held after a four-month period for a Namibian Constituent Assembly, which would create a constitution for the new country. South African police would continue to retain primary responsibility for law and order; other nonmilitary forces would be disarmed. The special representative would develop election procedures in conjunction with the administrator-general, and would approve all aspects of the plan.

Four requirements were established to define "free and fair" elections: the removal of remaining discriminatory legislation; the release of political prisoners prior to the election campaign; all Namibians outside the country were to be allowed to return; and, through the offices of the

United Nations High Commission for Refugees, these Namibians were to be given free choice as to whether they returned or not.

South Africa agreed to these proposals on 25 April, which placed the onus for making the proposals work on the United Nations and on SWAPO, which had a number of reservations. South Africa then mounted a major attack in early May on Namibians at Cassinga, 150 miles inside Angola, killing about five hundred. This was widely seen as an attempt to force SWAPO to pull out of the negotiations, and it was briefly successful, but the front-line states managed to keep SWAPO at the negotiating table.

By accepting the proposal of the Contact Group, South Africa had scarcely changed her position at all. The twelve-paragraph document was necessarily so broad that there was enormous scope for argument over interpretation. The agreed-upon deadline for a transition to independence was the end of 1978, which meant that the United Nations's force would have to arrive in Namibia in May. Clearly anyone who appreciated the logistical problems involved in collecting a multinational force, obtaining the approval of the host country as to its composition, and transporting it to Namibia could be confident that the timetable would slip substantially.

South Africa's early agreement therefore had the effect of putting everyone else in the wrong, and South Africa exploited this situation to the full. In September it denounced both SWAPO and the Security Council for delays (the latter had only ratified the proposals at the end of July). The letter also raised three key issues: that the administrator-general should continue to run the territory during the transition (so as to reduce the role of the special representative), that South African police would retain primary responsibility for law and order; and that the South African troop level would be reduced only after the cessation of hostilities.

These requirements were a bid to retain the status quo. Yet they remained within the letter of the settlement proposals. Earlier, South Africa had stressed its claim to the Walvis Bay enclave, quoting in its support a statement from the Conference of East and Central African States in Lusaka: "As far as we are concerned the present boundaries of the states of southern Africa are the boundaries of what will be free and independent African States." In July, Vorster threatened to pull out of the negotiations if a Security Council resolution was passed calling for the integration of Walvis Bay with the rest of Namibia but, although such a resolution was passed, the Contact Group managed to prevent South Africa from backing out.[8]

The other issues on which Pretoria attacked the Contact Group during 1978 included the alleged partiality of the United Nations, the size of the South African troop reduction, and the introduction in UNTAG's plans of 360 civilian police. South Africa criticized the United Nations for providing funds to SWAPO to enable it to maintain a New York office. Academically, there is considerable logic behind this criticism, but, once the decision had been made that SWAPO was the legitimate representative of the Namibians, it became necessary to provide the organization with sufficient support to enable it to compete diplomatically with a powerful sovereign state and with a government in Windhoek that enjoyed the full political and financial support of South Africa.

South Africa presented four main criticisms of the settlement plan as it developed through the remainder of 1978. The size and composition of the United Nations's force was repeatedly questioned; it was inevitable, however, that changes would occur as the task was defined in greater detail. South Africa particularly opposed the use of the 360 civilian police, although they would be well qualified to accompany the South African police forces in the discharge of their duties, which had been specifically noted in the settlement proposal. The South African objection was that civilian police might take a more restrained approach to law enforcement than would their South African counterparts and so might materially affect the pressure that could be applied on anyone who opposed South African interests during the transition period. Civilian police have a precedent in United Nations's operations: there is a contingent of Australians in the peacekeeping force in Cyprus.

South Africa further claimed that the administrator-general had not been sufficiently consulted as to the composition of UNTAG, on which Steyn was not likely to be expert. The main point of contention, however, was whether the elections, scheduled for December 1978, should be held regardless of the progress of negotiations. Slippage of the election date was inevitable for reasons already given. But, South Africa claimed that the date must remain fixed to avoid upsetting the expectations of the people of Namibia. The underlying aim of this demand was that, if negotiations were not concluded by that time, the cease-fire would not yet be in effect and South African troops could therefore be in complete control during the election period.

The special representative, Martti Ahtisaari, a Finn, visited South Africa in January 1979, accompanied by the commander-designate of UNTAG. They also visited the front-line states and Nigeria, and met with Sam Nujoma, SWAPO's leader. During these visits areas of disagreement were clarified. Arrangements for the return of Namibians were fairly easy to make, using the expertise of the United Nations High Commission for Refugees. Stumbling blocks remained over the implementation of the cease-fire and the restriction to base of troops on both sides. South Africa questioned the willingness and ability of Angola and Zambia to control SWAPO during this period (a reasonable doubt, given the difficulty that the MPLA had in controlling UNITA in southern Angola). Although South Africa continued to challenge the composition of UNTAG, this question had been almost resolved by March; the problem became one of holding the contributing countries to their commitments.

The Cassinga massacre led SWAPO to question the good faith of South Africa. This doubt was reinforced after the assassination of Chief Clemens Kapuuo, the Herero leader and president of the DTA, in 1978. SWAPO denied involvement, but Steyn introduced legislation to permit detention without trial, and those persons that he arrested were all supporters of SWAPO; Steyn's ability to maintain the distance he had appeared to have established between himself and Pretoria fell into doubt.

SWAPO was given additional cause for concern by the announcement by Vorster in May 1978 that, in accordance with the demands of the DTA in Windhoek, he would start the registration of voters in Namibia with or without the consent of the United Nations, unless the settlement were implemented soon. Vorster authorized registration as his last act before resigning in September, and elections were held in December. Considerable intimidation was alleged, and South African troops displayed their loyalties by placing DTA stickers on military vehicles. Over 80 percent of the population went to the polls, and the DTA gained forty-one of the fifty seats, but SWAPO and two other anti-South African parties boycotted the elections. Initially, these elections were put forward as a move toward an internally arranged independence, but Western opinion was so strongly against them that South Africa had to retreat and describe them as a domestic poll that demonstrated overwhelming rejection of SWAPO.

Once the DTA had won the election, the South African position changed slightly. In letters to the United Nations, South Africa began to stress the need to take into account the views of the "duly elected leaders of South-West Africa." The intention was clearly to develop the DTA as a de facto government independent of Pretoria. In a later exchange of letters, which prepared the way for the Geneva talks in 1981, South Africa insisted that the DTA should attend these talks on the same basis as other parties. The secretary-general was forced to concede that the Contact Group would meet with them, although he was unconvinced and recalled that South Africa had frequently stated that it retained authority in Namibia pending the settlement.

The year 1979 was one of changing fortunes for the Contact Group and for their negotiations. During January and February, South Africa seemed anxious to make amends for the December elections, welcoming a visit from the special representative in January and declaring itself satisfied with the proposals, except for minor details. Pieter W. Botha, the new prime minister, was proving to be less hawkish than many had expected. Western pressure mounted, and South Africa lost one of her few friends with the fall of the Shah of Iran.

By the end of the spring, however, the prospects for a settlement grew dim. A new Conservative government in London was determined to resolve the Rhodesian problem, and, when Lord Carrington convened the Lancaster House conference in September, Rhodesia became the overwhelmingly dominant diplomatic issue. Opposition within Namibia to a settlement grew during the year. South Africa had moved in May to turn the Turnhalle Alliance into a National Assembly with power to alter or repeal legislation passed in South Africa, implying a marked diminution of the powers of the administrator-general. When the Alliance subsequently repealed discriminatory legislation—by passing the Abolition of Racial Discrimination (Urban Residential and Public Amenities) Act—a right-wing white party threatened to use contacts in South Africa's own National Party to discredit Botha. He responded by removing Steyn and putting in his place Gerrit Viljoen, who was another liberal, but whose position as head of the Broederbond gave him great influence over conservatives in both South Africa and Namibia. On the day that further talks were due to start with the Contact Group in New York, the Security Council condemned a South African attack on SWAPO. Such an act was clearly not conducive to obtaining concessions from Pretoria, and the talks were inconclusive.

One major change occurred in 1979 in the terms of the proposal. President Neto of Angola proposed in July that both sides should observe a demilitarized zone along the border of Namibia with Angola and Zambia. By the end of the year, this concept was accepted, although details continued to be disputed. The zone was to extend fifty kilometers either side of the border, except in the Caprivi Strip, where the Namibia-Botswana border to the south would restrict it. Early in 1980, the new commander-designate of UNTAG visited the proposed zone and the countries concerned with implementing it. He was Prem Chand, an Indian general who previously had commanded the United Nations's peacekeeping force in Cyprus. Aside from a number of routine questions about the ability of UNTAG to control a zone of such size, South Africa was primarily concerned about the number of military camps that it would be allowed to maintain within the zone. They started with forty, but the South Africans were prepared to reduce this number by 50 percent, which was well in excess of the seven bases for SWAPO that Angola and Zambia envisaged and that were put forward as an ideal number for South Africa, as well. By June, however, both SWAPO and the front-line states had agreed to twenty South African bases in the Namibian part of the zone and also that there would be no SWAPO bases in Namibia.

South Africa continued to apply military pressure on SWAPO and tried to discredit the organization in the eyes of the United Nations. In February, Foreign Minister Roelof F. Botha warned of impending attacks on Namibia by SWAPO that were to be launched with support from the MPLA and the Zambian National Defence Force, and documented eighty-seven guerrilla attacks inside Namibia in the preceding three months. Angola countered with similar details of South African aggression across the Angolan border.

In June these raids flared into a major invasion of Angola by South African troops. Pretoria described the raid as "a small combat team with some air support" and categorically denied Angolan reports of one motorized brigade, two battalions of parachutists, and an armored-car squadron. South Africa claimed troop strengths of approximately 150; Angola put it at 2,500. South Africa reported that the leading elements of the "combat team" were withdrawing across the border on 27 June but only confirmed that their forces were entirely in Namibia on the 30th. The time taken for the force to cross the border suggests that the Angolan claim was fairly accurate.[9]

One of South Africa's main strategies has clearly been to weaken SWAPO as much as possible by military attacks on its bases in Angola. It can hardly hope to destroy a movement with such popular support among the Ovambo and with such widely dispersed leadership. But the destruction of SWAPO's military power would seriously erode its bargaining position and might either gain South Africa more time before independence or ensure that SWAPO's participation in supervised elections was not supported by guerrilla intimidation.

The result of the elections in Zimbabwe provided a reminder of how vulnerable negotiations were to external factors. The second half of 1980 was marked by further South African raids into Angola and by a focus in the negotiations on the question of the impartiality of the United Nations. This issue dominated the October talks between South Africa, Brian Urquhart (the United Nations's under secretary-general for special political affairs), and the commander of UNTAG. As a result, the secretary-general called for further "pre-implementation" talks to resolve the acute mutual distrust. They were held in January 1981 in Geneva.

Almost all of the substantive issues had been agreed to before the Geneva talks convened. The timetable envisaged a cease-fire in March 1981; the reduction of South African troops to 1,500; the restriction of armed forces to bases by June; and, after a four-month election campaign, United Nations's supervised elections in October to elect the Constituent Assembly that would determine the constitution of the independent state.

The talks collapsed. Ostensibly, the reason was that South Africa remained unconvinced of the impartiality of the United Nations, even though it was stressed that the settlement proposals would be directly under the aegis of the Security Council and not under other United Nations organizations—the General Assembly or the Council for Namibia—which were aggressively pro-SWAPO. South Africa countered that the Security Council approved funding for SWAPO and thereby indicated its support for their rhetoric. The United Nations also made it clear that, once the electoral campaign began, SWAPO would no longer need its support and so the two organizations would effectively move apart once they were both deployed in Namibia.

In reality, the talks foundered because Ronald Reagan was elected to the U.S. presidency. It was remarkably naive to have scheduled important talks in the period between the election and his inauguration. South Africa could reasonably expect a Republican president, who had campaigned on a hard line against Soviet expansion, to be more sympathetic toward Pretoria than President Carter had been. There was no incentive from that quarter to settle; and it had always been the consistent application of pressure by the West that had led to the modest progress that had thus far been achieved.

South Africa, content that the diplomatic initiative had stalled for some months, took other measures in January to strengthen its position before talks could resume. First, it set up the South-West Africa Territory Force, an indigenous army containing a large number of blacks. United Nations Resolution 435 referred specifically to the reduction and withdrawal of *South African* forces; the more indigenous troops that could be trained prior to the arrival of UNTAG, the more the elections could be manipulated to favor the DTA. The second move, which was designed to complement the formation of this army, was the introduction of universal conscription for all men between the ages of sixteen and twenty-five. This policy did away with previous racial restrictions on conscription, but South Africa seriously misjudged its effect. It concentrated the minds of many young blacks, and considerable numbers decided that, if they were going to have to fight, they would rather cross the border and join SWAPO.

Notes

1. In 1968 the United Nations renamed South-West Africa "Namibia." The name is not recognized by South Africa, which now uses the joint name South-West Africa/Namibia in its negotiations with the United Nations. In general, the name South-West Africa is used con-

cerning any event prior to June 1968, and Namibia is used in reference to more recent history.

2. For a full account of South Africa's administration of the mandate, see John H. Wellington, *South-West Africa and its Human Issues* (Oxford, 1967), 270–319.

3. For the definitive work on the legal history of the dispute between South Africa and the League of Nations, and later, the United Nations, which quotes *in extenso* from the records of the International Court of Justice, see John Dugard, *The South-West Africa/Namibia Dispute* (Berkeley, 1973).

4. *Mandate for German South West Africa,* League of Nations Document dated 17 December 1920.

5. Official Records of the United Nations General Assembly, Twenty-fourth Session, Annexes, Agenda Item 10b, Document A/7754 (New York, 1969), paragraph 11.

6. The teleological approach to international law holds that any instrument, such as a mandate, should be interpreted so as to give maximum effect to the intentions of the drafters. In contrast, the formalistic approach to law stresses the sovereignty of states and seeks to minimize the impact that a legal instrument can have upon that sovereignty. In 1966 the majority of judges were essentially formalistic and the dissenting judges teleological in their approaches to the case.

7. United Nations Document S/RES/385 (New York, 1976).

8. Ibid., S/12678, letter dated May 22, 1978.

9. Ibid., S/14028, letter dated June 27, 1980.

2 Political and Economic Realities in a Time of Settlement

Robert I. Rotberg

Solving the Namibian problem is the immediate preoccupation of the West in southern Africa. Only by transforming Namibia from a territory administered by South Africa into an independent nation by a lengthy process acceptable internationally can the wars in Namibia and Angola be brought to an end, and the threat of enhanced Soviet prestige and influence in southern Africa be eliminated.

When it came to power in 1981, the new U.S. administration boldly made settlement of the Namibian issue its prime African foreign-policy objective. The U.S. State Department decided that new, assertive tactics would succeed in bringing the contending parties together where the more cautious, piecemeal methods of the Carter administration had proved only incrementally helpful. Although, for South Africa, Namibia is a crucial line of defense, the policy of the Reagan administration was based on obtaining South Africa's cooperation, whether by persuasion or conviction. The new policy saw the accomplishment of peace and independence in Namibia as a means of containing communism and eliminating painful areas of local conflict and potentially serious threats to world order.

Yet a resolution of the Namibian question has proved, and will continue to prove, excruciatingly difficult, less because of anything intrinsic to Namibia than because Namibia is a proxy issue. Whether ultimately correct or not, South Africa fears that to give way substantially in Namibia would be to mortgage its own future considerably. Independent Africans often agree. For them, Namibia stands astride the path that leads from the coup in Portugal and the victory in Zimbabwe to the successful transformation of Pretoria and Cape Town. Western negotiators have traditionally (and appropriately) burked this issue. So does Security Council Resolution 435. But, for South Africa, it is the nagging question, with short-term domestic as well as long-term politico-strategic implications.

There was a time when South Africa's desire to keep control over Namibia was predicated on the notion that Namibia was intrinsically rich. No power in Africa has ever wanted to deprive itself of real or imagined resources. South Africa is self-sufficient in most respects, but has not yet found petroleum within its borders or under its coastal waters. The results of prospecting off the shore of Namibia, where there were once

29

high hopes of finding a continuation of Angola's oil-bearing deposits, have been disappointing. Although an American firm may some day find exploitable petroleum in the Etosha Pan in north-central Namibia, geologists would be very surprised.

Given an absence of oil and a slumping demand for most of the other minerals, South Africa no longer needs Namibia economically. Nor can it enhance its own international position as a mineral producer by combining Namibia's supplies with its own. Manganese, chromium, platinum, and vanadium are strategic metals found in South Africa. Of the four, only vanadium is mined or known to exist in Namibia, and in insignificant amounts.

For these reasons, Namibia is, on its own, no outstanding prize economically. Although larger than Germany and France combined, it is a land of emptiness set between two sets of major rivers. The Orange in the south divides Namibia from South Africa. The Kunene and the Okavango, in the north, provide the border with Angola. Other rivers and streams flow, but only seasonally, and a few run deep beneath the heavy sands that were deposited over Namibia, and over its minerals, in comparatively recent geological times. Much is rough and mountainous, and everywhere it is dry. The dunes near the coast are among the highest in the world and attractive to tourists. Only in the most northern fifth of the country, where about half of Namibia's 1.1 million inhabitants reside, is there water in any measure of abundance. There, in the land of the Ovambo, annual crops can be grown and some measure of subsistence assumed. Otherwise, Namibia is a country where the indigenous inhabitants have long grazed cattle or sheep and goats. Whites, and peoples of mixed background from South Africa, joined Africans in these pursuits in the nineteenth and twentieth centuries, and today they comprise about a fifth of the total population. The estimated population of Namibia, by ethnic group, is: Ovambo, 600,000; whites, 105,000; Kavango, 100,000; Damara, 93,000; Herero, 71,000; Nama, 45,000; Caprivi, 40,000; Coloureds, 38,000; Bushmen (San), 35,000; Basters, 25,000; Kaokovelders, 11,000; Tswana, 9,000.

Economically, Namibia has few resources aside from its minerals. Moreover, their potential should not be overemphasized, since much of what has been or is likely to be found in Namibia is highly price elastic. Gem diamonds, now suffering from a worldwide slump in demand, have in recent years provided about 40 percent of government revenues. Mined by Consolidated Diamond Mines, Ltd. (CDM), a Namibian subsidiary of South Africa's De Beers Ltd., the world's major diamond producer and marketer, they will probably continue to be the country's most valuable export until the end of the century.

Uranium oxide is the only other large resource. The Rössing Mine, near Swakopmund on the Namibian coast, is the largest uranium mine in the world. Approximately one-sixth of the free world's annual supplies comes from this mine, which since 1979 has been providing about 5,000 tons per year to Europe and the Far East. Although exempt from Namibian taxation for at least another year, the Rössing mine (owned principally by Rio Tinto Zinc of Britain) is soon expected to rival CDM as the country's largest generator of revenue and foreign earnings. Much of Rössing's production is fortunately committed by long-term contracts. At present low world spot prices, which are likely to prevail to the end of the century, mining the uranium of Rössing might otherwise prove uneconomic. Certainly there has been no rush to exploit Namibia's two other large known deposits of uranium.

Base metals are also mined in Namibia. The U.S.-owned Tsumeb mine has exported copper since the 1920s. It recently purchased another copper mine and also exports cadmium. There are small tin mines, a small zinc mine that shut down in 1982, arsenic, lead, and vanadium deposits that are now almost at the end of their working life.

Geologists are sure that Namibia contains additional base-metal resources. But, given the present marginal profitability of the copper mined in Namibia, and prevailing low world prices for most metals, it is unlikely that minerals will prove to be as much of a bonanza for the country as was once assumed. Unless petroleum is discovered (which is now thought to be very unlikely), or nuclear reactors again become popular, Namibia is not exceptionally rich. Although potentially wealthy per capita, by African standards, it is not intrinsically an area the possession of which would have overweening global value.

Until recently, Namibia exported sardines and pilchards, caught off its coasts, and grew the karakul (Persian) lambs that provided warm coats for the wealthy of the northern hemisphere. But the schools of sardines and pilchards were overfished and are no longer netted off Namibia. Sales of karakul have also declined as a result of a slump in West German demand. Potentially, chilled beef could be supplied to South Africa and the European Economic Community, but, aside from diamonds and uranium, Namibia is a property with few crucial resources.

Namibia's long coastline on the Atlantic Ocean is arguably of strategic importance, and a case could be made for the naval utility of Walvis Bay, the South African-owned port that is Namibia's only major transportation outlet. But no sophisticated analysis of likely Soviet attempts to intercede adversely against Western shipping would assign Walvis Bay that high a value. The existence of the coastline alone is not significant, nearly all of it being thoroughly inhospitable, with few anchorages and little but sand.

In cost-benefit terms, Namibia has two prime values, especially to

South Africa: as a physical buffer, and as a bargaining chip. Both notions are more psychological than real, another indication of the logical illogicality that has defied a rational solution to the Namibian problem.

In geopolitical terms, for example, it is easy to make a strong case for defending South Africa along the Orange rather than the Kunene River. In addition to the obvious fact that it runs on South Africa's own border, and not along disputed territory, the Orange River passes through arid, desolate landscapes where aerial reconnaisance is inexpensive and effective. Platoons create dustclouds that can be seen from miles away. Moreover, the indigenous population is largely non-African, speaking languages different from the potential infiltrators, and providing a much less receptive host population.

Along the Kunene and Okavango rivers in the north, by contrast, there is bush, the plains become waterlogged when it rains, and the inhabitants on both sides of the river are indistinguishable in appearance and language from the guerrillas. South of both rivers is Ovamboland; most guerrillas belonging to the South-West Africa People's Organization (SWAPO) are Ovambo and speak their language.

To wish to defend one's motherland along secure, legitimate frontiers makes sound military sense. But for several years the South African Defense Force has constructed massive encampments south of the Kunene and has successfully prevented Ovamboland from being overrun by the forces of SWAPO. The South Africans prefer to continue to defend themselves 1,000 miles from their own heartland, often even striking boldly across the Kunene into the southern marches of Angola.

The war has been contained along the northern reaches of Namibia; South Africa's military planners know that they can continue to do so into the foreseeable future. Why, they seem to ask the politicians, should they be compelled to press their backs against their own heartland? Such views will influence South African official thinking until either the cost of keeping 25,000 troops outside South Africa becomes too high, until those troops are needed elsewhere (perhaps at home), or until their masters see political benefits to be gained or international objectives to be accomplished by a tactical retreat south of the Orange River.

In the first half of 1982, South Africa claimed to have lost only 47 men (but twice as many as in the first half of 1981) to the guerrillas, and to have killed nearly 600 of their opponents (100 more than in the same period in 1981). SWAPO in Angola possesses surface-to-air missiles, but has not managed to put them to dramatic use. South Africa controls the skies and continues to play a role in supplying the Union for the Total Independence of Angola (UNITA), the anti-Angolan government insurgent group led by Jonas Savimbi. Neither Cuban nor Soviet assistance to the Angolan government seems to deter South Africa. Although it was true in 1982 that neither side could win on the battlefield, it was also true that South Africa continued to be militarily ascendant and largely unchallenged by SWAPO's smaller and less well trained guerrilla army.

In many ways, Namibia as a bargaining chip means more to South Africa than does its status as a military buffer. Official South Africa likes to play diplomatic poker, and plays the game well. Without Namibia, South Africa might have little with which either to tempt or to forestall the West. Endless to-ing and fro-ing over Namibia is to South Africa's advantage. Once Namibia is independent, South Africa will have lost an important psychological shield.

Although no side can afford to let negotiations reach an impasse, the Reagan administration's African policy has been predicated on an internationally valid Namibian settlement being achieved in 1982. White South Africa, however, is playing for high stakes—for what its present leaders believe (rightly or wrongly) to be its very survival.

For these reasons and others, it should be abundantly clear that the South African search for proper modalities since 1977 has been largely a way of extending the process of bargaining. By 1980, the Carter administration and South Africa had successfully eliminated all but a few technical obstacles in the way of a negotiated settlement. If there had been the will on the part of South Africa, the Reagan administration could easily have found ways to convince it that a Namibian ceasefire, electoral campaign, and poll could be conducted impartially, and the new state created.

In early 1981, when the South Africans undermined the Geneva meeting, their reason was a lack of faith in the objectivity and impartiality of the United Nations. But that was only the most convenient excuse. President Reagan's election, and the possibility that a Republican administration in the United States would not demand a transfer of power (or at least would negotiate, as it has, from scratch), was a powerful cause. So was Prime Minister Pieter W. Botha's desire to hold an early election in South Africa.

South Africa's reluctance to conclude a definitive settlement has been fortified by its fear that the winner of any comprehensive, fair election would be hostile as a neighboring government. Botha's South Africa has largely been unprepared to gamble. Even the example of Zimbabwe, where supposed Marxists—in the flush of victory and with the responsibility of developing an integrated state—have behaved like canny capitalists and have largely eschewed immoderation, has not encouraged South Africa to expect similar conduct from a postindependence Namibia.

The specter of a red flag over Windhoek has been used by Botha and his ministers to spread fear and despondency among whites, and—unwittingly and paradoxically—to make their own negotiations that much more difficult. In the South African lexicon, SWAPO, an admitted recipient of Soviet funds, arms, and support, has always been termed a communist terrorist organization. Official South Africa has therefore asserted that a SWAPO government would give bases to the Soviet Union and staging points to anti-South African guerrillas.

But there is an alternative hypothesis. Given the likely structural weakness of a future Namibia, it is difficult to argue that a new Namibia—whoever leads it—would be capable of operating much more stridently than has Zimbabwe or Botswana. Its infrastructure is tied closely to that of South Africa; its pool of trained local manpower is small (perhaps 300 university graduates compared with 15,000 in Zimbabwe); its economy is much less diversified than that of Zimbabwe and much more integrated into the economy of South Africa; Walvis Bay, its major port, is South African (at least until a new agreement is reached); and its white population is proportionally much larger (10 percent of the total in Namibia, only 3 percent in Zimbabwe).

Such arguments do not shake the South Africans. They refuse to credit the possibility that the government of a new Namibia would concentrate primarily on its own economic and political development, refraining from engaging in the kinds of adventurism that could incur South African displeasure. Botswana has long refused to afford anti-South African guerrillas permanent facilities. Zimbabwe has likewise denied bases to guerrillas. A new Namibia would be more fragile than either of these nations, and only a foolhardy regime would convert itself into a transit area for opponents of white South Africa. Even if it should do so, South Africa would be able to maintain a steady surveillance of the open areas in southern Namibia across which potential infiltrators would have to travel.

From about 1977 to early 1979, South Africa's negotiators were less constrained by uncertainty about the future of their nearby colony. Until then, and possibly until Robert Mugabe's overwhelming electoral triumph in Zimbabwe in 1980, many official South Africans believed that a SWAPO victory at the polls could be avoided. Their expectation was that the Democratic Turnhalle Alliance (DTA), led by Dirk Mudge, could win a majority, or, in combination with centrist parties, at least deprive SWAPO of the right to rule. Mudge, a stalwart of the Namibian branch of South Africa's National Party until the mid-1970s, emerged in 1976 as a far-sighted leader of the Turnhalle constitutional conclave. South African-sponsored, the Turnhalle was composed of nominated representatives from each of the country's ethnic groups, with the largest and the smallest having approximately equal representation. South Africa expected that the Turnhalle meetings would prepare a constitution for an independent Namibia that would enshrine ethnic equality (disregarding

Political and Economic Realities   35

population) and thus give whites a permanent position in Namibia greater than their numbers would normally allow. The Turnhalle was intended to give legitimacy to an internal initiative, albeit South African backed, which could preempt external guerrilla thrusts and gain support from the West.

The election of President Carter coincided with the conclusion to the Turnhalle exercise. Being persuaded by Western representations that the Turnhalle was a dead letter, Prime Minister B.J. Vorster of South Africa astonished Mudge and others in 1977 by aborting the exercise and virtually admitting, for the first time, that Namibia was a lapsed mandate and that South Africa's jurisdiction had, since 1945, been without foundation. But no internationally acceptable solution to the Namibian question was immediately agreeable to South Africa. In Namibia, Vorster urged Mudge to transform the various Turnhalle ethnic groupings into the DTA, which would then campaign politically against SWAPO. In late 1978, the DTA won an overwhelming electoral victory against only token, mostly white, opposition; SWAPO, being externally based, could not participate.

Since then, especially during the last three years, the DTA, in control of Namibia's national assembly, has conducted itself more and more like a territorial government. South Africa, ruling through an administrator-general, has steadily devolved power over all local matters except security, police, and foreign relations to Mudge's council of ministers. (A separate assembly only for whites is controlled by a hard-line National party affiliate, which complicates matters considerably, but Mudge has won most of the jurisdictional battles.)

Together, the DTA and the administrator-general have removed the legal backing for most forms of discrimination, especially barriers to the free movement of labor and to job advancement. Namibia now has no pass laws, no influx control, no statutory reserved jobs, and no legislated social segregation at the national level. Residential areas are theoretically open to all, as are hotels and restaurants. In practice, however, desegregation is incomplete, and white control of municipal affairs has perpetuated a color bar in the schools, hospitals, and swimming pools. But there is no denying that in Namibia, at least, social and economic apartheid is being eroded.

Mudge is dedicated to change. He also wishes to hasten development for indigenous Namibians. He wants both to govern effectively and be seen to govern effectively; he wants to come out from behind the shadow of the administrator-general and, as much as possible, from South Africa. He is forthright on these matters, believing that the DTA can only be a credible alternative to SWAPO if it shows itself to be truly multiracial, and truly pro-Namibian, with effective power. To Mudge's mind, the internal initiative in Zimbabwe (1979–1980) failed because Bishop Abel

Muzorewa never took the reins of government firmly into his own hands, and because he failed to unify all of the internal groups that were opposed to the guerrillas.

Mudge and South Africa contend that the DTA has a chance of winning an electoral contest with SWAPO only if the DTA can demonstrate its governmental effectiveness and mobilize support, especially among the Ovambo. But, in early 1982, these calculations were disturbed by the resignation of Peter Kalangula, the DTA's president. Kalangula, an Ovambo who was once an Anglican priest, denounced the DTA's determination to remain an ethnic coalition. He had tried to convert it into a fully national party instead of a congeries of ex-Turnhalle ethnic groups.

Without Kalangula, the DTA's appeal to the Ovambo will obviously suffer, as could its ability to project a credible national image. If the DTA's electoral viability is widely perceived to have been diminished, the entire basis of South African policy will have to be re-examined.

The DTA has long indicated that, when the election was finally announced, it would successfully woo SWAPO dissidents and the non-DTA, non-SWAPO, middle-of-the-road voters and groups who, at least theoretically, could help the DTA deprive SWAPO of a victory at the polls. Those middle groups, however, were much more opposed to the DTA and much more irrelevant in 1982 than they were in the 1970s. The Namibian National Front (NNF), once the major centrist party, functioned more on paper than in reality. Nominally, it brought together the South West African National Union (SWANU), a Herero-dominated, largely urban political entity; the Damara Council, which controls Damaraland; the white Federal party, largely a paper organization with few members; and other, more minor, organizations. SWAPO-Democrats, led by Andreas Shipanga, until 1975 a leading SWAPO official in Zambia, had a much reduced following. Kenneth Abrahams, a Coloured physician, ran the Namibian Independence Party, which also had few adherents. In 1982 it was apparent that there was no obvious political role for those Namibians who, although uneasy with a guerrilla struggle and distrustful of SWAPO, were even more bitterly opposed to South Africa and its DTA creation.

In 1982 few knowledgeable Namibians, South Africans, Americans, or Britons could conceive of a fair, internationally supervised election that would give much less than an overwhelming victory to SWAPO. However, because of that conclusion, the Contact Group (the United States, Britain, West Germany, France, and Canada, acting together) and South Africa had agreed (in Phase I of the negotiations between the West, South Africa, and SWAPO) that the constituent assembly, which was to be elected at the end of the pre-independence process, could adopt a national constitution only by an affirmative vote of two thirds of its members.

Subsequently, and much more controversially, the West and South Africa agreed to hold the national election using procedures similar to those employed in West Germany. Instead of straight proportional representation, with voters casting ballots for national lists of candidates (on the Israeli model), the U.S. State Department proposed that Namibians should each effectively cast two ballots, one for a national list, with seats in the constituent assembly to be allocated proportionally, and one for individual representatives in specific constituencies. Half of the seats in the assembly would thus be filled by each method. Depending upon how the constituencies were delimited (Namibia has never voted in this manner, and there has never been a full voter registration), the combination of proportional representation and constituency seats could conceivably assist the DTA, with its ethnic appeal, and frustrate SWAPO's ability to command an overall two-thirds majority.

SWAPO opposed such an election. Objectively, however, the combination of the two kinds of voting could as easily benefit SWAPO as not. Given what is known of voting in first-time elections in Africa, and of Namibia's historic antipathy to South Africa and everything South African, almost any fair method of distributing seats after the balloting is likely to result in a sizable SWAPO majority.

There have been no opinion polls. But the probability of a SWAPO triumph is predicated less on its ideological appeal than upon the widespread acceptance by most Namibians of SWAPO's legitimacy. Almost everywhere in Africa (and, in recent times, in southern Africa), indigenous voters have again and again cast ballots, when the opportunity presented itself, for that party that had waged the most effective verbal or military struggle against the oppressive colonial power. The result in Zimbabwe reinforces that view. So do very informal discussions with Namibians of all classes and colors. But it is the widespread acceptance in local circles of a SWAPO victory that, whether or not accurate, indicates that Namibians, like Zimbabweans and others before them, may be expected to vote for the party that is widely anticipated to triumph. Legitimacy in this context is greater than the sum of the parts of the struggle; there is an obvious desire to be aligned with the winning side.

Even were this rough calculation less widely perceived, the sheer arithmetic of Namibia argues in favor of a SWAPO sweep. Although SWAPO has many ranking Herero and Damara leaders, to name but a few of the peoples of the country, its top leadership is Ovambo, and most of its guerrilla cadres have been drawn from Ovamboland. This is as might be expected, since more than half of Namibia is Ovambo by ethnic affiliation and language. SWAPO began its life as an Ovambo organization; it is still widely perceived to be an Ovambo entity. As a start, SWAPO can hence probably be assured of massive Ovambo backing. Even before Kalangula's defection, the DTA had been unpopular in Ovamboland; its remaining Ovambo leaders have little Ovambo following. Moreover, the war has taken place in Ovamboland and has helped to mobilize the Ovambo in opposition to South Africa and the DTA.

In addition to this presumed heavy backing by half of the country, SWAPO can count on large-scale support from among the Damara (who have resoundingly refused thus far to vote for the DTA), and a measure, perhaps an overwhelming measure, of support from the Kavango (who live immediately to the east of Ovamboland), the Caprivi (who inhabit the curious peninsula separating Zambia from Botswana), the Nama (in the south of the country), and the Basters (a mixed-race group who live south of the capital). More modest support for SWAPO can be anticipated from the Herero and from a few of the 21,000 German-speaking whites. Turning the prism around, the DTA could in 1982 be assured of only some of the white votes (many would vote for neither the DTA nor SWAPO, but for a right-wing white alternative), some Herero votes, and a sprinkling from the other, mostly ethnic, smaller components of Namibia.

There is absolutely no guarantee that the non-Ovambo half of the country would cast its lot with the DTA; the Damara oppose the DTA, and anti-DTA parties have won recent elections in Namaland, in the Baster area, and elsewhere. Moreover, although such is an argument of silence, no amalgam like the one that Mudge leads has ever succeeded, when put to the test, in stemming the tide of perceived legitimacy in Africa. Nor can Mudge claim remaining credible black adherents or leaders.

South Africa has hitherto refused to let Namibia become independent mostly because it constituted a psychological buffer. The South African defense force may also believe, with a reasoning that is untested and obscure, that the fight against guerrillas is best kept as far away as possible from Pretoria. The ruling National party has feared the political consequences of a true devolution in Namibia: a SWAPO victory might unleash a white domestic backlash; a Marxist-dominated government would reign on the western flank of South Africa; Afrikaners fleeing from Namibia could vote for right-wing alternatives to the National party in crucial constituencies in the Transvaal; the National party's opponents could accuse the Botha government of selling out kith-and-kin; and so on. At one time, South Africa may have wanted Namibia for its resources, particularly uranium, but not now.

Economic considerations aside, that same logic remains powerful. Although Prime Minister Botha won a major test of strength against the right wing of his National Party in early 1982, his government is as a result more, rather than less, beholden to the political barons of the Transvaal. Botha, personally, may not want to risk another struggle with the right, and he may not want to antagonize the white electorate. If caution prevails, and the military are not anxious to settle, then only the pull (rather than the push) of U.S. (and Western) concern, and any concessions that can be wrung out of the Americans, can concentrate the minds of official South Africa sufficiently to lead to a permanent transfer of power to a representative government in Namibia.

As this is written, all sides are bargaining hard. The South Africans are attempting to ensure the impartiality of the United Nations and any international supervisory team and monitoring force. That is a rhetorical issue, but nevertheless one that all sides can dispute. There are questions about the absolute size of the United Nations military force and about the pre-electoral disposition and placement of SWAPO guerrillas. The conduct of the campaign, the registration of voters, delimitation of constituencies, and the detailed organization of the elections are under intensive discussion. So must be the delicate period of postelectoral transition. A constituent assembly will be elected by popular vote. Who will convene it? Who will run the country during this period? If South Africa, can it intervene to influence the deliberations of the assembly? Will South Africa be permitted to prevent the assembly from completing its work or to refuse to ratify any results that are decided upon by a majority short of two thirds? Assuming a smooth transition, who will declare and how will Namibia become independent?

However these questions are answered—and they must be—South Africa must also decide whether or not its own self-interest (including a potential domestic backlash and security considerations) has been safeguarded. Only if (and when) South Africa satisfies itself that SWAPO will lose, that the risk of a SWAPO victory is worth chancing, that a SWAPO government could be coopted or otherwise manipulated, or that the pressure from the West permits no further delays, will the long negotiations about Namibia's future be concluded and an irrevocable agreement, leading to elections and independence, be concluded. If not, the impasse will be prolonged.

The materials from which a settlement is ultimately constructed, the temper of the conflict that precedes it, and the duration of the interval between the impasse in 1982 and a conclusive cease-fire are all factors that are certain to influence Namibia's postindependence performance.

The attitudes of Africans and whites will depend, to a major extent, upon the bitterness of the final process of resolution, on the manner in which South Africa agrees or is compelled to withdraw, on the way in which the United Nations and South Africa assist or retard the transfer of economic as well as political power, and on the statements and actions that South Africa, SWAPO, and others make and take during the delicate days of decision, devolution, and finally, deliberation in the constituent assembly.

Namibia is fragile socially, economically, and politically. How its independence is inaugurated, and how the new state is organized, will depend on the composition of the structure bequeathed to the new nation. So, too, will it depend upon the leadership exercised by those who withdraw and those who assume power. The remainder of this book focuses upon those myriad critical considerations that will help to mold the precise form of Namibia's future.

3

The Economy in Transition to Independence

Wolfgang H. Thomas

In any speculation about postindependence Namibia, an assessment of the country's current economic state and its prospects during the transition to independence has to play a key role. This chapter examines Namibia's current socioeconomic situation and the structural realities that will shape its economy after independence.

In presenting such an overview, I have intended to display as little ideological and political bias as possible, or, at least, clearly to state the sociopolitical assumptions underlying alternative possibilities. This has also been my approach in *Economic Development in Namibia: Towards Acceptable Development Strategies for Independent Namibia* (Munich, 1978), which reflected the situation up to early 1978 and included detailed statistics, as well as a comprehensive bibliography. This chapter updates and revises some of the material of the earlier study, placing emphasis on recent economic trends and recognizing sociopolitical changes that have occurred since 1978.

For a small country with a population of just over one million people, the literature on Namibia is substantial. In addition to unpublished preliminary reports by governmental institutions and agencies in Western and socialist countries, mention must be made of the work by the German Institute for Development Policy, the Namibia Institute in Lusaka, the African Institute in Pretoria, individuals such as Murray, Collett, and von Kleist, and governmental planning bodies in Windhoek. As a result of these contributions—and a significant relaxation of controls over the release of statistics by authorities in Windhoek (in particular the Directorate of Finance)—our knowledge and understanding of Namibia's current economy is at present much better than it was a mere four years ago.[1]

Basic Characteristics of the Namibian Economy

Namibia is a land of contrasts, particularly in its geography and ecology, its heterogeneous societies, and its sociopolitical patterns. A vast land area of 823,168 square kilometers carries a population of just over one million (see table 3–1). Large stretches of desert and semidesert area in

Table 3-1
Population of Namibia: 1970–1980: Official Estimates

Ethnic Group	Census[a] 1970	Percent	Midyear Estimate 1979[a]	Percent	Midyear Estimate 1980	Percent
Black						
Ovambo	352,640	46.3	446,300	47.3	458,900	47.3
Damara	66,277	8.7	83,500	8.8	85,900	8.8
Herero	50,609	6.7	64,400	6.8	66,100	6.8
Kavango	50,103	6.5	63,700	6.7	65,400	6.7
East Caprivi	25,583	3.3	32,700	3.4	33,600	3.4
Kaokolanders	6,566	0.8	8,400	0.9	8,600	0.9
Tswana	3,830	0.6	4,700	0.5	4,800	0.5
Other	15,088	2.0	17,000	1.8	17,400	1.8
Brown						
Nama	33,007	4.3	42,200	4.5	43,400	4.5
Coloured	28,510	3.7	32,700	3.4	33,500	3.4
Rehoboth Basters	16,646	2.2	20,700	2.2	21,400	2.2
White						
Afrikaans	62,290	8.2	69,700	7.3	71,300	7.3
English	8,345	1.1	9,400	1.0	9,600	1.0
German	15,955	2.1	17,800	1.9	18,200	1.9
Other	3,327	0.5	3,700	0.4	3,800	0.4
Bushmen	22,786	3.0	29,100	3.1	29,900	3.1
Total	761,562	100.0	946,000	100.0	969,800	100.0

[a]Latest revision by the Department of Statistics.

the southern and coastal regions contrast with semiswamp conditions in parts of the northern regions, below the Kunene and Okavango rivers. Promising agricultural and mining exports (karakul, cattle, diamonds, uranium, and copper) and a relatively small, although highly sophisticated, commercial sector of the modern economy stand in sharp contrast to the subsistence agriculture practiced in most of the northern regions, as well as in other so-called tribal areas. The "white' city of Windhoek, with its superb urban infrastructure, contrasts sharply with the nearby Coloured and black (largely residential) townships of Khomasdal and Katatura, and even more dramatically with smaller towns and villages elsewhere in the country.

Namibia's only efficient and well-equipped harbor suitable for international sea traffic is not situated within the country, in as much as Walvis Bay falls outside Namibia's present territorial boundaries. The picture becomes even more complex if we take into account the ethno-cultural heterogeneity of this small population: eleven ethnic groups are distinguished, ranging from the numerically dominant Ovambo to the few remaining San (Bushmen). Even within one group—the whites—we find no less than three well-entrenched language groups: Afrikaans, English, and German (see tables 3–2 and 3–3).[2]

The Physical Infrastructure

It has often been stated that, considering the vastness of the area and the sparseness of the population (1.4 persons per square kilometer), the country has a relatively well-developed physical infrastructure. There are more than 3,500 kilometers of tarred roads (the latest project being the Tsumeb-Rundu road that stretches northeast across Kavango to the Okavango River), and about 30,000 kilometers of gravel roads. Road-building and maintenance services are efficient, although in the black areas of the north and in the other so-called homeland regions roads are generally poorly developed.

Direct links (a 2,340-kilometer rail line) exist between Walvis Bay/Swakopmund on the coast, Tsumeb in the north (south of Ovamboland), Gobabis in the east, the Cape border with South Africa in the south, and Windhoek in the center. The railway bus-service network covers 9,000 kilometers. Windhoek, Keetmanshoop, and Walvis Bay have large, modern airports capable of accommodating jumbo jets. Most other towns have smaller airports or strips. About 100,000 passengers are transported per year. Grootfontein and Ondangwa are the major military airports in the north. Upington, on the South African side of the Orange River, is the alternative refueling airport for South African flights on the way to

Table 3–2
Geographical Distribution of Namibia's Population, 1977

Region	Estimated Population
Northern region	665,000
Kaokoland	8,000
Ovambo	510,000
Okavango (including refugees)	110,000
Caprivi	37,000
(Rate of urbanization: ± 5 percent)	
Central region	355,000
Urban areas	
Greater Windhoek	100,000
Walvis Bay-Swakopmund-Arandis	35,000
Other urban areas	40,000
Rural areas	
Herero (eastern and western regions)	40,000
Bushmen	30,000
Damara	70,000
Tswana	8,000
Coloured	10,000
White	22,000
(Rate of urbanization: ± 50 percent)	
Southern region	80,000
Oranjemund	10,000
Rehoboth	18,000
Namaland	30,000
White	12,000
Other group/villages	10,000
(Rate of urbanization: ± 35 percent)	
Total	1,100,000

Source: Author's estimates.

Europe, the United States, and Latin America, if Windhoek is not available. Lüderitz in the far south has a proper harbor—which is, however, hardly utilized. Walvis Bay has a well-developed deep-sea harbor with facilities for passengers, freight, tankers, fishing, and naval defense.

Postal services are efficient; the telephone system encompasses about 50,000 subscribers; telegraph and telex services connect the urban centers and are closely linked to South Africa, with direct connections to Western Europe and to North and South America. Since 1979, the South-West Africa Broadcasting Corporation has provided multilanguage radio and television services, although with much reliance on South African programs.

The country has no significant energy resources of its own. Generators use coal, oil, and hydropower; the Van Eck power station in Windhoek is still the key supplier of electricity. Due to the war in the north, the

Table 3–3
Ethnic Structure of Namibian Population, 1980 Estimate

Ethnic Group	Estimate A	Percent	Estimate B	Percent
Ovambo	608,000[a]	51.0	470,000	44.8
Kavango	119,000[b]	10.0	112,000	10.7
White	98,000[c]	8.2	88,000	8.4
Damara	93,000	7.8	85,000	8.1
Herero	71,000	6.0	80,000[d]	7.6
Nama	45,000	3.8	54,000	5.1
Eastern Caprivi	40,000	3.3	40,000	3.8
Coloured	38,000	3.2	46,000	4.4
Bushmen	35,000	2.9	27,000	2.6
Rehoboth Basters	25,000	2.1	31,000	3.0
Koakovelder	10,700	0.9	–	–
Tswana	9,500	0.8	7,500	0.7
Total	1,192,200	100.0	1,050,000[d]	100.0

Sources: *Estimate A:* Author's medium-level estimate, based on various sources and the following assumptions:

[a]Temporarily absent "refugees" or "guerrillas/terrorists" included.
[b]Angolan refugees semipermanently settled in Kavango included.
[c]Nondomiciled members of the defense force included.

Estimate B: Alternative estimate prepared for the South-West African government in 1981.

[d]Kaokovelders included under Herero.
[e]9,500 "others" included. They constitute the missing 0.9 percent in the table. Another 0.1 percent is due to rounding.

hydroelectric power station at the Kunene (along the Ruacana Falls) can be used only occasionally. As an alternative, a link with the South African (ESCOM) electricity grid at Aggenys in the northern cape is currently being completed at a cost of about R 80 million. All supplies of oil and coal have to be imported from South Africa or elsewhere, resulting in very high electricity and fuel costs.

The lack of water at reasonable cost constitutes the single most important impediment to Namibia's rapid economic development. In addition to the three perennial rivers—the Orange, the Kunene, and the Okavango—as well as dams, boreholes, and semidry river beds, impressive plans have been worked out for piping water long distances from the Kunene and Okavango in the north to the major urban areas and mines in the south, and for the large-scale desalination of seawater. The development of these new water-supply sources is of particular importance as a precondition for opening up the new large-scale mining ventures. The high cost of water makes irrigation agriculture virtually impossible.

In the few major towns like Windhoek, Tsumeb, Keetmanshoop, Walvis Bay-Swakopmund-Arandis, and Grootfontein, the urban infrastructure is well developed, especially in the white townships. But the absence of larger urban agglomerations in the black homelands (in particular in the more densely populated Ovambo-Kavango-Caprivi region) has prevented the further development of an urban infrastructure. New towns like Oshakati have a restricted urban core, and the border war, the drought, and the establishment of fortified central places have resulted in the evolution of a new pattern of urban growth in the northern part of the country.

The main problem with Namibia's physical infrastructure is that it benefits the different regions and population groups unequally. The white-oriented structure of the past need not persist if all facilities are opened to people of all racial groups. However, the financing and operation of infrastructure services in Namibia are still highly dependent on South Africa. Negotiations with South Africa over the transfer of infrastructural facilities must thus be of crucial significance in the transitional phase. Providing a more equal distribution of these facilities, and future difficulties in obtaining funds for the maintenance of existing services, may cause a decline in standards.

Development Potential and Constraints

The prospects for Namibia's future development are difficult to evaluate. This fact has resulted in widely diverging opinions about its future, and a highly polemical, rather than factual or analytical, approach in much of the literature. Some observers have described the country as poor in resources, economically unstable, and hampered by nature. Others have described it as having one of Africa's best resource endowments relative to the size of its population. As an aid to presenting as comprehensive a perspective as possible, table 3–4 lists Namibia's major development assets and constraints.

Demographic Characteristics

Official estimates of Namibia's current population suggest a total of about one million in 1981; alternative estimates made in 1977 by SWAPO-oriented scholars put it at 1.25 to 1.5 million. I have in the past taken a medium estimate of 1.1 million for 1978 and 1.19 million for 1981 as a base for reference. For alternative estimates, as well as regional and ethnic breakdowns, see tables 3–1, 3–2, and 3–3. To update these estimates, an official census was undertaken during August 1981, but only preliminary results were available in 1982.

Based on my own population estimates and on more recent unofficial

Table 3-4
Development Assets and Constraints for Namibian Socioeconomic Development

Development Assets	Development Constraints
Natural Resources	*Natural Resources*
Existing	*Existing*
1. Minerals: diamonds, copper, uranium, zinc, and so forth.	1. Semidesert nature of large parts of the country.
2. Agriculture: export cattle, karakul pelts, wool, game.	2. Severe shortages of water; low rainfall and only three perennial rivers (Orange, Kunene, and Okavango).
3. Offshore fishing.	3. Lack of fuel resources (oil, coal, gas) and iron ore.
Potential	*Potential*
4. Expansion of mining: more uranium, iron ore, oil, coal, and so forth.	4. Depletion of mineral resources: diamonds, copper, and so forth.
5. Utilization of new water and energy resources (Ruacana: nuclear energy).	5. Depletion of fishing resources.
6. Intensive crop farming in Kavango, Caprivi, and part of Ovamboland.	6. Decline in agricultural potential due to erosion/overexploitation.
Structural Factors	*Structural Factors*
Existing	*Existing*
7. Developed infrastructure: physical, administrative. social, financial, and so forth.	7. Low population density (diseconomies of small scale) and limited local markets.
8. Low overall-population density.	8. Long distances and high transport cost.
9. Balance-of-payments surplus.	9. Extreme structural heterogeneity (ethnic and regional).
10. Close link to a highly developed economy (South Africa).	10. Inequality in the access to resources and the distribution of income and wealth.
11. Sophisticated modern sector in the local economy (skills, entrepreneurship, capital).	11. High degree of economic dependence on South Africa.
	12. Conventional development problems:
Potential	a. Extremely high export dependency of the economy.
12. Scope for a widening of the economic base:	b. High rate of population growth and rapidly increasing unemployment.
a. developing agriculture and consumer-oriented industries in the north.	c. Lack of skilled black manpower and efficient management.
b. processing raw materials.	d. High dependency on foreign development capital (largely South African).
c. selective import substitution and protection.	13. Increased risk and uncertainty due to pending independence and political polarization.
d. tourism.	
e. utilizing new water and energy resources.	

Table 3-4 (continued)

13. Economic advantage of an integration of the economy (de-balkanization).
14. Potential for increased tax revenues from mining sector.
15. Diversification of foreign-aid and trade links.
16. Scope for a selective expansion of economic cooperation in southern Africa.
17. Growth stimulation through an incomes policy and dynamic manpower development.

Potential
14. Severe political instability during and after independence.
15. Withdrawal of white capital, expertise, management, and so forth.
16. Unstable world-market prices and a declining demand for exports (karakul, diamonds).
17. Military conflict in southern Africa.

Source: Thomas, *Economic Development in Namibia: Towards Acceptable Development Strategies for Independent Namibia* (Munich, 1978).

figures, the following conclusions may be drawn. The white population was estimated at 105,000 in 1977/1978, which included about 31,000 households and 42,000 economically active persons. These figures did not include non-Namibian white members of the defense forces, who substantially increase the white presence in the country. During the past three years, the proportion of temporary residents has increased while the total white population has decreased substantially. First results of the 1981 census put the resident white population at only 75,000.

In 1977, the population of the northern region constituted about 60.5 percent of the entire population; the share of the total Ovambo population (including Ovambo resident in central and southern Namibia) is probably also greater than 50 percent (see table 3–2).

No detailed information is available about the age breakdown of the population. Table 3–5 suggests the following pattern for the total population, including a projection for 1990.

Namibia displays most of the demographic characteristics associated with Third World African countries—swift population growth and high dependency ratios. Numerically, the white group plays a relatively more important role than in any other African country except South Africa, its share of the total population being, for example, more than twice as large as that of whites in pre-independence Zimbabwe. As far as ethnocultural diversity is concerned, the Ovambo group is distinctly dominant, so that even a political coalition of all of the other groups would probably be unable to attain a majority of votes in an ethnically biased "open" election. However, the numerical domination of the Ovambo is not large enough to enable ethnic-oriented Ovambo leaders to count on a landslide election victory such as Mugabe achieved in Zimbabwe.

Table 3–5
Estimated Age Breakdown of the Namibian Population, 1977 and 1990

Age Group	Percent	Estimates for 1977	Percent	Estimates for 1990
0–4	17.0	187,000	14.0	238,200
5–14	29.5	324,500	29.0	493,000
15–19	10.5	115,500	10.7	181,800
20–44	30.2	332,200	31.2	530,500
45–64	9.8	107,800	11.5	195,500
65+	5.0	33,000	3.6	61,100
Total	100.0	1,100,000	100.0	1,700,000

Source: Author's estimates.

Labor Supply and Employment

Estimates of Namibia's labor supply and employment structure are equally difficult to determine, given the diversity of estimates for the total population. Tables 3–6 and 3–7 give the estimated structure of the labor force by sector and by occupation for the years 1978 and 1981.

My own estimates of Namibia's total labor force in 1981 suggest a figure of about 417,200 (that is, 35 percent of 1,192,000), where two-thirds of the force are men and one-third are women. Tables 3–6 and 3–7 set open unemployment at 40,000 in 1978, or approximately 10 percent of the labor force. Concealed unemployment or underemployment, which is very widespread in peasant agriculture and in the self-employment sector, could easily have amounted to another 40,000 to 50,000, thus pushing the rate of broadly defined unemployment up to about 20 percent of the labor force in 1978.

Taking into account an overall population growth rate of approximately 2.7 percent per year, with about half of the population below the age of seventeen, the average annual growth rate of the labor force could be close to 4 percent—that is, about 16,000 per year—since 1978. A

Table 3–6
Sectoral Employment Structure, 1978 and 1981

| | 1978 | | | |
Sector/Category	Blacks	Whites	Total	1981
Agriculture	–	–	185,500	
Commercial farming	44,000	6,500	–	46,500
Peasant farming	135,000	–	–	133,000
Fishing	5,000	500	5,500	3,500
Mining	19,500	4,000	23,500	24,500
Manufacturing industry	7,000	2,000	9,000	9,800
Construction	10,000	1,000	11,000	13,000
Electricity supply	1,400	250	1,650	1,800
Water supply	1,600	550	2,150	2,200
Transport and communication	7,500	4,500	12,000	13,000
Commerce, finance, and related services	17,000	5,000	22,000	25,000
Domestic servants	10,000	–	10,000	8,500
Social and community services	11,200	4,700	15,900	16,500
Government administration and services	6,800	7,000	13,800	15,200
Self-employed in black areas	26,000	–	26,000	24,000
Defense force	7,000	5,000	12,000	13,500
Unemployed and unspecified	39,000	1,000	40,000	65,000
Total	348,000	42,000	390,000	415,000

Source: 1978 figures are derived from official estimates and the author's calculations. The 1978 labor force is estimated as 34.5 percent of the 1978 population. 1981 figures are based on the author's calculations.

Table 3–7
Employment by Occupational and Skill Categories, 1978 and 1981

Category	1978 Blacks	1978 Whites	1978 Total	1981 Total
Agriculture:	–	–	185,500	
Commercial farmers	1,000	6,000	–	5,000
Farm workers	43,000	500	–	41,500
Peasant farmers	135,000	–	–	133,000
All other sectors:				
Managerial, technical, professional (teachers, medical staff, and so forth)	6,000	14,000	20,000	19,000
Clerical, secretarial, supervisory	4,000	7,000	11,000	14,000
Artisans and apprentices	8,000	4,000	12,000	14,000
Operators and semiskilled	36,000	4,000	40,000	42,000
Unskilled workers	33,000	500	33,500	35,500
Self-employed in black areas	26,000	–	26,000	24,000
Domestic servants	10,000	–	10,000	8,500
Security forces, police, and so forth	7,000	5,000	12,000	13,500
Unemployed and unspecified	39,000	1,000	40,000	65,000
Total	348,000	42,000	390,000	415,000

Source: 1978 figures based on the author's calculations. The labor force is estimated as 34.5 percent of the 1978 population (1,100,000 + 2.5 percent). The 1981 figures are also based on the author's calculations.

more conservative estimate, which allows for temporary (illegal) emigration of blacks, a shift of some economically active persons into the defense force, and a lower total-population figure, would put the annual increase in the labor force at 8,500.

To assess the overall employment situation in 1981, I suggest (for lack of more detailed statistics) that, due to the deteriorating economic situation, total employment in the various sectors has changed as follows:

Changes in Employment Opportunities: 1978–1981	Net increase (+)/ Net decrease (–)
Commercial farming	–4,000
Fishing	–1,500
Mining	–2,000
Manufacturing	± 0
Construction	+2,000
Commerce	± 0
Domestic service	–1,500
Self-employment in black areas	–2,000
Peasant farming (net of defense recruitment and emigrants)	–2,000
Government administration	+1,000
(A) Subtotal: Persons requiring alternative employment	10,000

52   Namibia: Political and Economic Prospects

Taking into account the increase in the labor force, as well as initial un(der)employment, the following overall picture emerges:

	Labor force increase at 2 percent per year for 1978–81	
(B)	(3 × 8,500)	25,500
(C)	Unemployment, 1978	40,000
	Total unemployment, 1981 (A)+(B)+(C)	75,000
	Estimated 1981 Labor Force	415,000
	Rate of unemployment, 1981	18.1%
	Un- and underemployment, 1981	75,000 + 40,000
	Rate of un/underemployment 1981	27.7%

Notwithstanding the tentative nature of these figures, the deterioration in the employment situation should be clear. At 18 percent, Namibia's rate of unemployment is at a critical level, as is the more broadly defined rate of un(der)employment at 27.7 percent. These figures are corroborated by other, more directly visible, evidence, such as the southward movement of black Namibians, rural uprooting in the north, a significant influx of people to the few larger towns, and the interest taken in recruitment to the defense force.

Assuming that the existence and seriousness of the employment problem requires no further elaboration, the employment challenge facing Namibia can be summarized as follows. Employment opportunities need to be created for at least 9,000 people per year, to take into account the annual increase in the local labor force. Gradually, as many as possible of the approximately 75,000 unemployed Namibians have to be absorbed, in addition to 40,000 "underemployed" persons and those individuals who are now being released from the peasant agriculture sector. The influx of people into the major towns has to be accommodated (physically and economically). Earnings of the poorly paid and the underemployed must be increased.

Present Growth and Development in Perspective

Namibia's Gross Domestic Product and Real Growth

Although figures for gross domestic product (GDP) only give a limited view of a country's economic growth and development, they can furnish an initial overview of long-run trends. Table 3–8 gives official estimates of the Gross Domestic Product for 1960, and selected years in the 1970s up to 1980. At current values, GDP increased at an impressive rate, rising

Table 3-8
Growth of Namibia's Gross Domestic Product, 1960–1980
(rands, in millions—at current prices)

Sectors	1960	Percent	1970	Percent	1973	1975	1977	1979	1980	Percent
Agriculture, forestry, fishing	20.5	14.6	49.7	15.5	76.4	112.2	111.8	110.8	128.1	9.6
Mining	47.6	33.8	105.1	32.6	184.1	159.9	349.2	578.8	632.7	47.7
Manufacturing	12.7	9.0	16.7	5.2	35.1	35.8	40.3	50.5	56.6	4.2
Electricity and water	—	—	3.7	1.2	5.1	8.7	15.1	21.3	26.3	2.0
Construction	5.7	4.0	14.3	4.5	18.0	25.3	32.3	35.9	38.8	2.9
Trade, catering, and accommodation	17.2	12.2	32.8	10.2	45.3	60.4	73.5	83.5	99.1	7.5
Transport and communications	12.0	8.5	24.6	7.7	36.2	48.9	51.6	71.8	76.7	5.8
Financial services	12.3	8.7	27.4	8.5	42.6	55.6	67.4	85.9	94.1	7.1
Community, social, and personal	1.5	1.1	5.6	1.7	7.5	10.1	13.3	16.5	18.6	1.4
General government	8.8	6.2	30.7	9.6	45.1	58.1	74.5	103.2	120.0	9.0
Other producers	2.6	1.9	10.5	3.3	15.8	20.8	27.0	32.8	37.1	2.8
Total	140.9	100.0	321.1	100.0	511.2	595.8	856.0	1,191.0	1,328.1	100.0

Source: Compiled and consolidated by the Department of Finance, Windhoek. Figure for 1960 from Africa Institute *Bulletin*, xi/xii (1981) table 5.

from R 140.9 million in 1960 to R 321.3 million in 1970 and R 1.327 billion a decade later. However, taking into account price increases and population growth, Namibia's per-capita GDP at constant (1970) prices developed as follows:

1960	R 324
1970	R 453
1975	R 446
1976	R 450
1977	R 415
1978	R 389

These per-capita figures indicate that average living standards actually declined in the 1970s. If one bears in mind that the salaries of civil servants and other persons in the modern sector of the economy did not decline during the 1970s, these figures suggest an even sharper drop in real living standards in the subsistence, or peasant, sector. The latter trend is, however, partially countered by the fact that peasant and informal sector incomes may be underenumerated in official GDP estimates.

The breakdown of Namibia's GDP by sector clearly reveals its relatively unbalanced economic structure; mining constitutes almost half of the total. During the two years up to 1980, the nominal increase in GDP was less than the rate of inflation (6.8 and 8.96 percent compared to inflation at 12 to 13 percent), so that real GDP growth was, in fact, negative. In light of the virtual denuding of the cattle-grazing area due to the drought, and to relatively slack diamond, uranium, and base-metal prices, the prospects for a positive real growth rate in 1982/1983 are equally bleak.

Notwithstanding these signs of stagnation and retrogression, Namibia's per-capita gross domestic product compares well with that of other African states of similar population size (see table 3–9). These comparative figures are, however, misleading in as much as income inequalities are far greater in Namibia than in the other countries on the list. For example, in 1975, average annual household income of whites in Namibia was the equivalent of $9,415, as compared with $2,448 among urban black households, and $578 among black households in the rural subsistence areas.

Sectoral Development

To assess the prospects for Namibia's future economic development and its relationship to sociopolitical factors, we now look at each of the major

Table 3–9
Comparative Per-Capita Gross Domestic Product, 1977–1978
(in U.S. dollars)

Country	Gross Domestic Product	Population (million)
Swaziland	$ 590	0.5
Botswana	620	0.8
Congo Republic	540	1.5
Liberia	460	1.7
Lesotho	280	1.3
Malawi	180	5.7
Namibia	1,012	1.1

Source: World Bank, *World Development Report 1980.*

subsectors. At stake are trends and issues concerning employment, modernization, living standards, and structural changes.

Agriculture

Agriculture plays a central role in Namibia's economic development. It provides employment or a subsistence income to about half of the total labor force; it contributes about 10 percent to overall GDP and 10 to 14 percent to exports; and it constitutes virtually the only economic activity in the northern part of Namibia and in some of the other areas set aside for the indigenous population.

Available statistics on the pattern of agricultural production are summarized in table 3–10. Livestock farming contributes about 98 percent of the gross value of commercial agriculture. Among the livestock products, cattle and karakul made up about 80 percent in the 1970s. In northern Namibia, mohango and sorghum are the staple foods. Aside from these crops, Namibia imports from South Africa the bulk of its basic food products such as maize, wheat, milk and dairy products, vegetables, fruit, and virtually all processed foods. In years of drought, large amounts of fodder for livestock are also imported.

A broad distinction can be made between modern commercial farming—which is largely limited to the white-owned farms, a part of the Rehoboth farming area, and a few farms owned by blacks elsewhere in the country—and the more traditional or subsistence farming in the black areas. There is a startling disparity between these two sectors in the relationship between output value and employment. In the modern sector, which provides about 80 percent of all commercial agricultural production, about 5,000 to 6,000 white proprietors employ about 44,000 workers, whereas about three times as many people are engaged in the subsistence sector.

Table 3–10
Agricultural Production, 1960–1980

	1960	1970	1975	1976	1977	1978	1979	1980
Gross output value								
Total (R '000)	34,516	65,518	111,398	135,847	120,431	123,515	152,785	183,700
Beef	17,665	33,185	54,676	62,985	55,198	62,676	77,564	—
Mutton	2,203	4,321	10,336	10,505	10,440	10,407	12,674	—
Karakul pelts	8,478	20,989	33,352	46,378	37,055	31,119	45,097	—
Wool	889	263	1,792	2,637	2,856	3,243	2,281	—
Other products	5,281	6,760	11,242	13,342	14,882	16,070	17,169	—
Production								
Karakul pelts ('000)	1,976	3,594	3,031	2,787	2,866	2,645	3,017	—
Wool ('000 kg)	4,576	3,592	4,498	5,026	5,092	4,871	—	—
Maize (t)	6,318	9,820	12,292	12,163	8,594	9,239	—	—
Millet (t)	34,569	32,727	35,800	41,596	40,295	25,000	24,000	—
Hay crops (t)	3,066	—	30,371	28,767	26,227	24,404		
National herds								
Cattle ('000)	2,440	2,934	2,464	2,566	2,854	2,619	2,620	—
Sheep ('000)—*Total*	3,132	4,700	4,203	4,256	4,502	4,140	4,188	—
Karakul	2,695	4,043	3,519	3,473	3,658	3,309	3,300	—
Other	437	657	684	783	844	831	898	—
Goats ('000)	1,359	1,585	1,564	1,571	1,621	1,612	1,810	—
Stock exports and slaughtering								
Cattle sold			326,064	389,248	348,734	396,952	420,189	460,072
Cattle exported on hoof			249,729	250,869	199,757	239,994	228,857	236,435
Local cattle slaughtered			76,335	128,379	148,977	156,958	191,332	223,637
Processing purposes			48,823	93,214	115,175	123,545	162,767	185,613
Other			27,512	35,165	33,802	33,413	28,565	38,024
Small stock slaughtered			314,335	290,948	275,951	252,757	248,081	204,050

Source: Directorate of Finance, Windhoek.

The Economy in Transition to Independence

Namibia's agricultural production is highly sensitive to annual rainfall, export prices (that is, world-market prices or prices attained on the South African market), marketing quotas and marketing efforts, and the efficiency of farm management. The standard of services (veterinary and pest control) and the availability of short-term credit, as well as long-term finance, also play a major role in the achievement of high productivity in commercial agriculture.

During the last few years some important changes have taken place in the agricultural sector. First, the devastating drought—in some areas lasting more than four years—has led to drastic reductions in livestock. Some places suffered a 50-percent loss of livestock during the 1980/1981 season. Due to attractive cattle prices (which reflect the scarcity of red meat in South Africa rather than internal market conditions) farmers have been encouraged to sell. In the black areas, the drought (and, in some parts, the war) have also led to large-scale cattle losses. These stock losses are likely to reduce future output levels for a number of years, a development that is welcomed by those observers who have for years warned against overstocking. In the south, the combined effects of the drought and a slump in overseas karakul prices have had an equally devastating effect on the size of sheep stocks. The drop in the stock on commercial farms has also had a dampening effect on black employment, which had already been declining in the modern farming sector.

Second, there has been a sudden boom in land prices, triggered by the injection of funds into black second-tier governmental authorities, many of whom have used a major part of the money to buy up formerly white-owned farmland. Although many whites have taken this opportunity to sell, others have used the income generated from cattle sales to buy more land. Thus, a declining number of white farmers own relatively larger farms, whereas black land ownership is increasing gradually, and is initially in the hands of only a few privileged farmer-politicians. In terms of both attempting to maintain agricultural output and achieving the long-run goal of socially beneficial land reform, this special type of "land redistribution" is counterproductive. It intensifies the class polarization, which is at the basis of the black/white conflict.

Third, marketing channels have been centralized in Namibia and are tightly linked to South Africa. This applies in particular to the marketing of cattle and karakul. Fourth, government subsidies and special "drought aid" to the largely white commercial-farming sector have increased during recent years, whereas the effectiveness of financial and other assistance awarded to the peasant sector has improved only marginally.

The short-run prospects for increases in output and employment in commercial agriculture are, therefore, poor. Uncertainty regarding the country's political future will probably cause more farmers to leave or merely to maintain past production levels and steadily repatriate capital to South Africa. No training efforts have been undertaken among black farmers to guarantee output levels on the land taken over from white farmers.

Seen in broader perspective, this situation spells disaster for Namibia's commercial agriculture in the long run. Ecological factors call for a high level of competence and a relatively high capital intensity in modern farming, while sociopolitical factors are leading to a gradual exodus of competent farmers, and an even more rapid outflow of private capital, without the substitution of non-Namibian expertise by local, trained persons. The lingering atmosphere of political uncertainty makes it impossible even to start recruiting competent expatriate farmers who might be willing to stay on in a postindependence Namibia, while the spreading war in the north (in particular, in the Tsumeb-Otavi-Grootfontein triangle south of the old "police line") continues to limit the use of the best cattle-ranching area.

As far as peasant agriculture is concerned, the position is little better. Problems and obstacles in the development of traditional agriculture include:

1. Limitations of nature
    a. Low rainfall; periodic droughts
    b. Shortage of irrigation water and boreholes
    c. Unsuitable soil structure; overdependence on livestock farming; danger of sand erosion
    d. High frequency of stock diseases

2. Structural Factors
    a. Long distance to markets and urban centers
    b. Poor transport and communication links
    c. Inadequate marketing channels
    d. Tribal communal landownership
    e. Lack of electricity and other basic services
    f. Lack of development finance

3. Demographic Factors
    a. Low land/man ratio (injustice of land allocation)
    b. Distorted age/sex ratio of labor force (migrant labor)
    c. High rate of population growth in rural areas
    d. Virtual absence of urban centers in peasant areas
    e. Restriction on migration to relieve overpopulation

4. Knowledge Gap
    a. Ignorance about alternative or supplementary products

The Economy in Transition to Independence

    b. Lack of acquaintance with improved methods and technologies; reluctance to innovate
    c. Lack of research and insufficient research transmission
    d. Isolation from modern agricultural sector and its demonstration effect
    e. Insufficient education/training facilities and lack of managerial skills

5. Inadequacy of Development Efforts
    a. Distrust of development corporations
    b. Overdependence on external assistance
    c. Lack of grassroots motivation and modernizing agents
    d. Shortage of funds for development projects
    e. Political instability, distrust of the bureaucracy and lack of any local agricultural pressure groups

Under the present sociopolitical climate, and given an economic system that emphasizes modern, white-controlled commercial agriculture and mining, the prospects for more immediate improvements in peasant agriculture are not good, notwithstanding all of the efforts made by the regional or ethnic development corporations—as well as some steps initiated by the defense forces.

It has been shown elsewhere in Africa that modernization efforts with respect to peasant agriculture presuppose some degree of national motivation, which itself requires a high degree of solidarity between the peasant population and the government in power, a situation that is hardly attainable in the northern area of Namibia under the current government. This far-reaching impediment has for years applied to Ovamboland, the most populous region in northern Namibia, but, as a result of the spreading war, it now also applies to Kaokoveld, the sparsely populated region in the northwest, as well as to Kavango in the northeast. For reasons more closely linked to the remoteness of the areas, but also related to the escalation of the war, rural development efforts in the Caprivi strip have been equally unsuccessful. In this regard, developments during the years before independence in Zimbabwe (and in Mozambique) have direct relevance for Namibia's northern rural areas: rural development has become a part of the "war of liberation." The fact that some parts of these areas (like northern Kavango) have a relatively high agricultural potential if properly worked, and might one day even produce a food surplus, is of little immediate relevance. Many of these factors also apply to the tribally allocated agricultural areas in the central and southern regions (the Herero, Damara, and Nama areas), except that their short- and long-run potentials are even more limited than those of the north.

This pessimistic conclusion concerning development prospects in the densely populated rural areas of Namibia is of great political significance. It points toward a vicious circle out of which the present "internal" government may not be able to escape, even though the issues and necessary reform steps are well known: effective sociopolitical mobilization of the rural population is a precondition for successful integrated rural development, which itself is a precondition for the economic advance of those regions. But, without such economic advances, the government cannot gain the political allegiance of the peasantry. With the current government's image of traditional elite domination, and with SWAPO being regarded as the modernizing revolutionary force, such a sociopolitical mobilization would be difficult, if not impossible, to bring about. At the same time, the one potential, although not optimal, alternative—large-scale southward emigration of the rural population—is also impossible due to the narrow employment base of the modern economy and to the protectionist policies of the present small urban elites.

I am not suggesting that a SWAPO-dominated (or any other non-DTA) government would easily, or successfully, solve this dilemma of lagging rural development. The rest of Africa is suffering from such development problems in the dominant peasant sector. Yet, under a different administration, failures would not be linked so directly to the sociopolitical structure of the government as is now the case. Sociopolitical mobilization may be easier—and some of the key obstacles (like the system of land use, the dominance of conservative chiefs, and the lack of dynamic rural-development training) may be overcome more successfully—by a broader-based, populist government.

In both commercial and peasant agriculture short-run prospects are gloomy as far as output, employment creation, and income-generation are concerned. In the longer run, prospects for steady improvement are equally gloomy under the present sociopolitical system, as the war of liberation continues.[3]

Fishing. Namibia's fish resources along the Atlantic coast have been economically significant in the past but, due to indiscriminate exploitation by foreign and local fishing companies, annual quotas of pelagic fish (pilchards and anchovies) had to be reduced drastically from a maximum of 940,000 tons to less than 200,000 tons in 1979, and only 138,000 tons in 1980 (see also table 3–11). As a result, the fish-processing industry in Walvis Bay—the only major industry in the area—had severely to reduce its production from ten million cartons of canned fish in 1975 to 920,000 in 1979. To protect its fish resources, South Africa and Namibia extended their fishing zones from 12 to 200 nautical miles in 1979, and a comprehensive research and conservation policy is being implemented.

Table 3-11
Output in the Fishing Industry, 1969-1980

Fish	1969	1975	1976	1977	1978	1979	1980
Total catch ('000 tons)	858	759	572	403	414	325	241
Pilchard	676	545	447	194	45	28	—
Anchovy	180	194	94	125	360	259	—
Red eye/mackerel	2	11	11	1	—	13	—
Maasbanker	—	9	20	83	9	25	—
Processing:							
Fishmeal ('000 tons)	203	147	106	75	160	79	—
Fish oil ('000 tons)	45	28	19	13	28	28	—
Canned fish[a]	4,395	10,779	9,698	3,991	1,149	920	—

Source: South African Shipping News and Fishing Industry Review, in: STATS (December 1979). Output for 1980 supplied by the Directorate of Finance, Windhoek.

[a] '000 cartons of approximately eighteen kilograms each.

Nevertheless, it is doubtful that annual catches will recover more than partially within the next few years. The situation was so critical in 1980 that the fishing season had to be cut short in spite of very low quotas. Some indications point to a recovery of the sardine stock, and canning is being resumed in 1982. Nevertheless, the situation remained depressed, with the fishing industry only contributing 1 percent to Namibia's 1980 GDP.

The collapse of the fishing industry has two important consequences. First, it has reduced the economic significance of Walvis Bay, the South African enclave along the coast of Namibia, which may now be more of an economic liability than an asset for South Africa (even though it is still of vital strategic importance, in particular for the transitional period to full independence). With recovery at best a slow process, the major fishing companies, most of which are South African-owned and controlled, may put less pressure on governments in Windhoek and Pretoria to protect their source of revenue. Second, the loss of several-thousand job opportunities in the canning factories has made Namibia's employment problem even more severe.

Mining. Namibia is known to possess a relatively wide range of minerals, including diamonds, uranium, arsenic, lead, cadmium, zinc, and copper in significant amounts. A number of other minerals are available in relatively insignificant amounts, and there are alleged, but as yet unproven, deposits of a few other minerals like coal, iron ore, and platinum. More recently, there has been speculation about oil deposits in the Orange River mouth area off the Atlantic coast and in the Etosha region, south of Ovambo. However, the bulk of all marketable output comes from only a few minerals, with diamonds mined at Oranjemund, and uranium extracted at Rössing near Swakopmund together constituting about 80 percent of total output value in 1980 (see table 3–12). No figures are published on uranium production, but I estimate that in 1980 the output was in the order of R 350 million, resulting in a total mining-output value of close to R 1 billion.

Diamond production reached its highest physical-output level in 1978. The mine has operated on a three-shift basis since 1978, and resources are put at fifteen-years production. Diamond prices surpassed a relatively high level in 1977/1978; in 1980 and 1981, prices were substantially lower, resulting in a decline of this subsector's contribution to GDP and tax revenues.

Rössing's initital capacity has been put at about 5,000 tons of yellow cake annually, but alterations to the plant have made it more flexible. In the light of the serious world-wide uranium glut that has been building since 1976 and the drastic fall in world spot market prices, earlier forecasts

Table 3-12
Value of Mining Output, 1970–1980
(rands, in thousands)

Mineral	1970	1972	1974	1975	1976	1977	1978	1979	1980
Total diamonds	63,043	88,537	121,590	144,599	178,659	354,186	417,737	382,632	398,932
Total copper	32,282	29,078	45,637	40,466	45,092	48,216	53,884	69,612	69,813
Blister copper	27,914	20,920	40,500	40,288	44,951	48,210	53,884	69,612	69,813
Copper concentrates	4,368	8,158	5,137	178	141	6	—	—	—
Total lead	14,998	13,419	24,528	17,930	16,421	20,543	24,357	32,818	32,710
Refined lead	11,757	11,553	22,682	15,298	13,559	18,467	23,418	32,818	32,710
Lead concentrates	1,500	1,070	489	484	609	534	—	—	—
Lead/vanadium concentrates	1,741	796	1,357	2,148	2,253	1,542	939	—	—
Total zinc	4,701	7,495	15,814	14,551	13,476	11,185	9,546	11,719	8,218
Zinc concentrates	2,997	4,301	7,188	5,398	7,563	6,905	6,744	8,334	6,309
Zinc oxide	1,148	2,108	5,379	5,994	5,913	4,280	2,802	3,385	1,909
Zinc silicate	556	1,086	3,247	3,159	—	—	—	—	—
Other minerals	5,191	4,451	4,648	6,963	16,721	24,381	35,406	48,269	68,948
Total (excluding uranium)	120,215	142,980	212,217	224,509	270,369	458,511	540,930	545,050	578,621

Source: Directorate of Finance, Windhoek.

of Rössing's rapid expansion and the opening of new mines (Langer Heinrich and Elf Aquitaine) may prove to have been overoptimistic, even though the bulk of Rössing's production is still sold on the basis of long-term contracts. Output values for uranium may, for some time, stabilize at about R 350 million. Rössing's eventual contribution to tax revenue (after all capital investment has been written off) has been estimated at about R 100 million at the current capacity level. This sum represents almost as much as all of the taxes levied on the diamond-mining sector in 1981/1982 (which have been estimated at R 124 million; see table 3-15, below).

Production and output values of other base metals recovered between 1979 and 1981, but no spectacular increases are expected in the near future. Of particular significance has been the acquisition by Tsumeb Corporation (controlled by Newmont Mining) of a 70-percent interest in the Otjihase copper mine, which was developed by Johannesburg Consolidated Investments near Windhoek, but was closed in 1977. The mine reopened in 1981 and was expected to reach full production in 1982.

There has for a long time been international interest in exploration for new mineral deposits in Namibia, but, in the light of international political pressure, the current war-like atmosphere in parts of the country, the desire to leave future options open, and the shortage of water for any major new mining venture (at least until additional piped supplies are ready), only a few of the interested parties have so far started exploring. This situation has concerned the current government, leading to implicit warnings that unutilized mining rights might be forfeited. These warnings are the logical consequence of the apparent paradox between the promising mineral resources and sluggish mining development coupled with the extreme concentrations of mining output in the existing diamond and uranium mines. In 1980 about 80 percent of Namibia's mining output, 45 percent of its GDP, 75 percent of its export value, and approximately 50 percent of government revenue, came from only two mining companies—Consolidated Diamond Mines, Ltd. (CDM) and Rössing Uranium, Ltd.—which therefore constitute not only economic and sociopolitical assets but serious risks as well, both for the present situation of the country and for its pre- and postindependence development.[4]

Of equal significance for the country's present and future development is the fact that this strategic mining sector employs only about 5 percent of the labor supply—although at wage and salary levels far above national averages. Conveniently secluded in the far-off mining towns of Arandis and Oranjemund, the two mining giants have developed a labor elite of some 15,000 workers, whose living standards are atypical of the country as a whole, although migrants channel some benefits to relatives in the more distant rural areas. In a paradoxical way these two impressive mining centers are both well prepared for and highly exposed to a radical change in the country's political structure. As enlightened and well-paying employers, they feel only limited pressure from local trade unions, yet, as symbols of "high-profit multinationals," they constitute a ready target for political and economic pressure.

Industry and Construction. Namibia's manufacturing sector contributed less than 10 percent to the country's GDP, and its share declined to only 4.2 in 1980 (see table 3–8, above). Real output has declined significantly in recent years. If Walvis Bay is included in GDP, the share contributed by this sector increases to about 7 to 8 percent because of the fish-processing factories. When they were in full production, the output of these factories represented 70 percent of the sector's gross output, 90 percent of its profits, and more than half of the total industrial employment.[5]

Aside from the processing of fish and agricultural products (for example, abattoirs), there are only a few relatively small industries, which include beer breweries, furniture and clothing factories, metal and engineering works, and other assembly plants. Manufacturing is insignificant at present and its role is unlikely to change as long as no deliberate industrialization strategy is put into effect for Namibia and the close ties with South Africa persist in the form of unrestricted entry and indirect protection for South African goods as a result of import duties vis-à-vis third countries. The Economic Advisory Committee, appointed in 1977 to assess Namibia's development potential, summed up the position of the country's industrial sector as follows: "Because [existing] types of industrial activities are largely place-bound, and are therefore dependent on external factors (for example, the availability of fish), it may be concluded that SWA/Namibia's industrial development in the past did not in itself constitute an integral part of the economic development process. There is no evidence that the economy was able, in the past, to establish any viable industries on a noteworthy scale. For a country with the economic structure of SWA/Namibia this is not unusual."[6]

Although more critical development specialists might dispute this blanket conclusion concerning Namibia's industrialization potential, it is a fact that the country lacks most of the preconditions necessary for a dynamically expanding industrial sector: its markets are extremely small; the population is scattered over a vast area; the country lacks energy resources and other industrial raw materials; there is no significant skilled industrial labor force; and capital, as well as entrepreneurship, would have to be imported. Yet, it is also a fact that little effort has been made by past governments to stimulate local industries.

In the long run, the more densely populated northern areas offer some opportunity for small-scale, labor-intensive (market-oriented) agro-industries, particularly if a normalization of relations with Angola makes it possible to utilize the market potential on both sides of the Kunene/Okavango rivers and if peasant agriculture develops. Such prospects are, however, unrealistic under the present sociopolitical system and in light of the existing animosity between Angola and Namibia.

The contribution of the construction sector to GDP and employment has fluctuated widely during past years, never reaching much more than about 5 percent of GDP and 4 percent of employment. Since the mid-1970s, when most of the large-scale infrastructure projects were completed, the relative significance of this sector declined steadily. The development of new mines and the defense infrastructure remained the major stimulating demand factors. If the present uncertainty about Namibia's sociopolitical future continues, the position of this sector is unlikely to improve, even though public-sector spending for housing, hospitals, and schools continues to rise rapidly under the present government due to its efforts to satisfy the material needs of the electorate. More recently, private residential construction has increased again in the urban areas, although public-sector spending has suddenly been impeded in some spheres (for example, municipal housing), as a result of budget constraints.

In relation to its small population and vast area, Namibia's physical infrastructure is already of exceptionally high standard. Rising government revenues, efforts to stimulate employment and overall economic activity, defense demands, and the general quest for efficiency have all interacted to keep infrastructure standards high, notwithstanding uncertainties about the country's future. Difficulties with respect to the hydroelectric power scheme at Ruacana have resulted in the implementation of a R 80 million high-priority transmission project that will link Namibia to South Africa's power grid. Rail links with South Africa are being modernized; new tarred roads are being built; and water-supply facilities near Walvis Bay/Swakopmund are being expanded and supplemented by long-distance pipelines from the Kunene/Okavango.

Given adequate government revenues and a minimum level of sociopolitical stability, it is to be expected that further expansion of the physical infrastructure will continue to receive high priority under the current government, with emphasis gradually shifting toward the construction of housing and social infrastructure facilities. Yet, as the preindependence experience of other countries has shown, the political benefits of such social development projects will probably be limited so long as the population at large does not accept the legitimacy of the ruling government.

In the long run, future developments in industry, construction, and the physical infrastructure will depend primarily on such factors as investors' confidence and the availability of public funds. Prolongation of the war, as much as a radical change in government combined with an exodus of private investors, is likely further to hinder development in these sectors, even though short-term factors like the demand for accommodations by the staff of any transitional United Nations' team could temporarily enliven investment prospects.

Other Economic Sectors. Economic activities in the remaining sectors—commerce; catering; transport and communications; professional, social, and community services; and general government—although significant in their contribution to GDP and employment (see tables 3–6 and 3–8, above), are largely dependent on the growth and development of the key sectors discussed previously. Close links with corresponding sectors in South Africa have kept their size at a minimum, which is true of not only the more specialized commerce, finance, and communication sectors but also of the more sophisticated professional and social services. As long as such ties continue, overall economic growth in Namibia remains relatively low, and no deliberate steps are taken to indigenize these sectors, they are not likely to expand rapidly. Tourism may be taken as an example: political uncertainties, the effect of the war and the lack of a comprehensive tourism strategy (to which is related the reluctance of the government and local authorities to desegregate recreational and tourist facilities) combine to prevent dynamic growth in this sector. It is now little more than an appendage of South Africa's tourist industry, even though some local firms operate successfully and the country has its own distinct tourist attractions.[7]

Overall Assessment of Economic Performance

By considering the structure, potential, and interrelationships of all of the sectors, it is possible to arrive at an overall assessment of the current economic situation and of long-run development potential (leaving aside political factors at this stage). On the whole, the economy is stronger than those of many other southern and central African countries (see comparative data in table 3–14) and its performance in terms of the growth in GDP, government revenues, infrastructural development, exports, and household income has been impressive during the past ten to fifteen years.

Balance of Payments. Namibia's trade balance has shown a significant surplus during recent years, due to high levels of diamond production

Table 3-13
Comparative Social-Development Indicators

Country	Area (km²)	Projected Population 1977 ('000)	Population Density 1977 (km²)	GNP Per Capita 1977 (R)	Budget 1978–1979 (R m)	Agriculture's Contribution to GDP (%)
Botswana	600,372	715	1	385	207	29
Chad	1,284,000	4,000	3	115	70	50
Congo Republic	342,000	1,400	4	435	241	12
Ethiopia	1,221,900	29,300	24	95	672	48
Gabon	267,667	505	2	3,245	1,132	13
Lesotho	30,355	1,200	39	200	138	37
Mauritania	1,030,700	1,300	1	235	50	23
Niger	1,267,000	5,000	4	140	226	51
Namibia	823,140	974	1	944	520	17
Swaziland	17,363	515	30	505	169	28
Zambia	752,614	5,300	7	390	895	13

Country	Literacy (%)	Students 1975–1977 (%)	Population Per Doctor 1975–1977	Population Per Hospital Bed 1975–1977	Population Per Kilometer Tarred Road	Population Per Kilometer Railways	Population Per Telephone 1975–1977
Botswana	18.4	22.5	9,250	317	3,270	1,060	110
Chad	5.0	5.6	41,970	1,181	1,490	8,000	600
Congo Republic	28.8	31.7	7,315	201	4,515	1,750	115
Ethiopia	10.0	4.1	73,040	3,307	—	26,665	370
Gabon	14.8	28.5	2,580	124	2,520	775	45
Lesotho	56.5	19.3	18,655	488	6,000	400,000	290
Mauritania	11.1	5.5	14,000	2,569	2,320	2,000	—
Niger	11.0	4.1	42,620	1,390	9,025	—	590
Namibia	35.0	22.1	4,570	126	290	390	20
Swaziland	20.0	22.4	9,200	290	2,265	2,300	60
Zambia	47.7	19.8	10,375	260	1,765	2,425	100

Source: Adapted from Africa Institute, *Bulletin*, xi/xii (1981), table 13.

Table 3–14
Balance-of-Payments Estimate
(Rands)

Source	1977		1980	
1. Exports		694		1,023
Agricultural products	135		255	
Fishing	50		30	
Mining	509		738	
2. Imports (excluding defense goods)		−521		−756
3. Trade balance		+173		+267
4. Services balance		− 83		−127
5. Government transfer[a]		+ 55		+ 78
6. Net-factor payments		−140		−184
7. Balance on current account (3+4+5+6)		+ 4		+ 34
8. Capital movements		−100		−150
9. Net balance (7 + 8)		− 96		−116

Source: Figures for items 1 through 7 obtained from the Directorate of Finance, Windhoek. Item 8 is the author's estimate. The export figure is relatively low, in light of mining-output data for 1980.

[a]Defense expenditure of South Africa in Namibia excluded.

and sales, and the rapidly rising export value of uranium (see table 3–14). Compared to the performance of these two main export products, the sluggish trend in agricultural exports, fishing, and other minerals is of less significance. However, the increasing dependence on only two export products—both of which are sensitive to fluctuations in world prices, marketing channels, and politics—is a limiting factor. In addition, the balance of payments is burdened by an increasing rate of profit repatriation, food and other imports, and by imports of defense goods. These weaknesses have, together with a large-scale outflow of capital, interacted during recent years to turn Namibia's net balance of payments into a deficit.

Government Revenues. During the last ten years, Namibia's budget has gone through a difficult period because spending on large infrastructural projects was not financed by rapidly rising government revenues from local sources. Taxes from diamonds were virtually the only significant input, given the decline in fishing, sluggish agriculture, low base-metal prices, and the fact that no tax revenues have yet been collected from Rössing. This situation should change beginning in 1983, as tax revenues from uranium mining increase rapidly and soon contribute substantially to overall government receipts. The recovery of some other base-metal prices should also increase revenues, although this income will be offset by lower diamond taxes due to declining exports.

However, the prospects are not as bright as they appear at first sight. (For a breakdown of the 1981/1982 budget see table 3–15). Apart from

Table 3-15
Namibia's Central Revenue Fund, 1981-1982

Revenue estimates	Rands	Percent
1. Taxes and duties on diamonds	124,251,000	15.2
2. Taxes on other mines	1,000,000	0.1
3. Taxes and loan levies on companies	24,740,000	3.0
4. Nonresident shareholders tax	15,000,000	1.8
5. General sales tax	40,000,000	4.9
6. Other taxes	2,700,000	0.3
7. New loans	120,000,000	14.7
8. Capital repayments and interests	3,430,000	0.4
9. Licenses, fines, forfeitures	3,527,000	0.4
10. Departmental revenue	18,738,000	2.3
11. Post and telecommunications revenue	30,870,000	3.8
12. Customs and excise	250,000,000	30.5
13. Contribution by South Africa for 1981-1982	50,000,000	6.1
14. Compensation by South Africa for services transferred	134,000,000	16.4
Total	818,256,000	100.0

Major Expenditure Categories	Rands	Percent
1. Constitutional development	42,185,000	5.2
2. Finance (including transfer to 2nd/3rd-tier governments)	310,164,000	37.9
3. Civic affairs and manpower	23,630,000	2.9
4. National education	24,690,000	3.0
5. Economic affairs	23,910,000	2.9
6. Justice	5,270,000	0.6
7. Agriculture and nature conservation	80,460,000	9.8
8. National health and welfare	26,608,000	3.3
9. Water affairs	46,440,000	5.7
10. Central-personnel institution	1,660,000	0.2
11. Post and telecommunications	32,190,000	3.9
12. Transport	95,620,000	11.7
13. Defense	59,710,000	7.3
14. Police	44,950,000	5.5
15. Audit	580,000	0.1
Total	818,256,000	100.0

Source: Budget estimate, Windhoek.

mining taxes, most other revenue sources are likely to increase very slowly (if not decline), even in the medium term. The widening of the revenue base by extending taxation to all black households will have only a minor effect. The present government found it necessary to reduce income-tax rates for the upper income groups to prevent the loss of skilled workers to South Africa. A closer look at Namibia's 1981/1982 budget indicates that, of a total projected income of R 818.1 million, internal resources (taxes, loans, and departmental receipts) only cover about 46.9 percent (R 384.3 million), which already includes a relatively large amount of R 120 million—one-third of the total—that is to be raised by way of loans coming from South Africa and overseas. The remainder is made up of direct or indirect transfers from South Africa, including a R 250 million allocation for customs and excise. The total amount of R 818.1 million includes R 60 million for defense, which undoubtedly is only a small fraction of South Africa's total expenditure on the border war (for which amounts of approximately R 350 to 500 million per year have been cited). South Africa's annual financial commitment to Namibia may at present be close to R 1 billion.[8]

The amount that in future will be transferred from South Africa is an unknown factor of some significance. A movement toward greater regional autonomy may result in lower subsidies of regular activities (notwithstanding a far higher overall transfer) if Namibia's own defense spending and other items which were hitherto fully financed by South Africa, are taken into account. It may then be difficult for the Namibian government to fund social-development projects, even with higher tax revenues from mining. This problem was already in evidence in the 1981/1982 budget, which left only limited scope for broad-based development activities. The prospects for 1982/1983 are viewed with even more distress by the DTA government, which is very conscious of the effect its budget can have on electoral support.

Household Earnings. Available data show significant increases in the past few years in average wage levels and nonwage remuneration in the mining and manufacturing sectors and, to a lesser extent, even in paid farm and service employment. This development has pushed up real household earnings and consumer spending, a trend that should continue with rising export prices (although possibly at a slower rate due to the drought and other recessionary factors). However, paid employment reaches less than half of the black labor force, and the relatively high rate of inflation has limited real gains. Higher wages have led to more capital-intensive production at a time when no sectors in the economy are able to absorb redundant labor.[9]

In sum, the Namibian economy is still booming, but the boom rests on shaky foundations, which are likely to erode in future. If the political status quo continues, a number of dampening factors are likely to combine to reduce substantially the prospects for growth. However, a rapid transition to internationally recognized independence would introduce other factors that would also dampen economic activities.

Trends in Social Development

The concept of "social development" is used here in its wider sense, relating as much to the sphere of the individual (for example, the improvement in living conditions), as it does to society as a whole. However, to narrow the scope of this section, I limit the discussion to only four important issues: the elimination of discrimination; manpower and the administrative infrastructure; education and training; and the improvement of the social infrastructure, including housing, health, and social welfare. Only the most important factors and forces will be considered.

Eliminating Discrimination. Much of the pressure behind the independence movement in Namibia stems from the strong desire by black Namibians to have all forms of racial discrimination abolished. This urge relates to the sphere of labor and employment as much as to property rights and the use of community or cultural amenities. In all three spheres, significant progress has been made during the past five years to abolish formal racial discrimination, and some, although only limited, steps have been taken to implement nonracialism. Statutory job reservation and the limitation of black workers' rights have been abolished, the migrant-labor system has been made more flexible with respect to the migrants' right to stay in urban areas, and other restrictive regulations concerning training have been lifted. The principle of "equal (nondiscriminatory) pay for equal work" has also been widely accepted, and concern for the payment of at least minimum wages has increased. Yet, the implementation of these principles through every sector of the economy and every enterprise is a slow process. Results are at present uneven. The emphasis that has been placed on ethnic differentiation in politics and regional development has hampered the movement toward nondiscrimination, since differentiation is often a substitute for traditional discrimination. In particular, for second-tier government activities (including education, health, cultural services, agricultural development, and regional administration), the system of ethnic differentiation has entrenched discriminatory treatment. In contrast, the principle of affirmative action has hardly been accepted by the white elite that dominates the labor market.[10]

Success is even more difficult to gauge in the area of property rights, notwithstanding the lifting of certain restrictive regulations. Blacks are now allowed to buy property in the formerly all-white areas of towns like Windhoek (although not in Walvis Bay) and a few individuals actually have done so. The same right formally applies to the acquisition of industrial and commercial properties, although financial constraints and the scarcity of such items for sale have largely prevented any effective "encroachment" of black entrepreneurs upon central business districts. In the all-black townships, the acquisition of property by prospective tenants has been impeded primarily by factors other than discrimination, resulting in only slow progress. It is legally possible to acquire freehold tenure in the tribal areas and agricultural land in the white areas, but in actuality the process is very slow. The acquisition of farming land by blacks outside the tribal areas has been facilitated by the funds made available to second-tier governments.

Finally, the pace at which community and cultural amenities initially established only for whites have been opened to all races has also been unequal. This issue constitutes one of the main points of conflict between the DTA central government and the National party-dominated white administration, which controlled most of these amenities in the past. Municipal libraries have been opened, but public swimming pools have not. With the resurgence of white conservatism during the past eighteen months, the process has slowed, and bitterness has increased among blacks.

So long as the present DTA government remains in power, and South Africa is responsible for the military protection of the country against SWAPO insurgents, it is unlikely that the current slow process of integration will be accelerated. This fact is likely further to exacerbate black-white antagonisms on which the war of liberation is, in the final analysis, based.

Manpower Needs and the Administrative Infrastructure. Several studies have been undertaken in the past to assess the manpower implications of Namibia's transition to independence. The conclusions invariably depend upon assumptions made about the future role and presence of skilled whites in the country and the extent to which emigrating whites would have to be replaced by local blacks or expatriates. Although it is beyond the scope of this chapter to review or revise past estimates of manpower replacement needs, a few general points can be made about this important issue.[11]

First, white skilled and semiskilled manpower is already leaving Namibia at a steady pace. Census results for 1981 show a 25-percent decline in the white population. Farmers are selling their land and moving to South Africa; only a relatively small percentage of school leavers and students remain in the country or return from study abroad; and there has been an exodus of local authority staff (town clerks, treasurers, and engineers) for whom the long-term possibilities for employment or re-transfer to South Africa are not assured. In the private sector, the rate of labor turnover has increased during recent years, with a larger percentage of those currently employed keeping open a "fall-back" position in South Africa. This applies even more to the civil service, where earlier moves to force white officials to choose between secondment status and permanent employment petered out, probably because of opposition by a majority of individuals in the service to such a clear-cut choice. As the bulk of white civil servants allegedly support the National party of South-

West Africa (and favor close ties with South Africa), it can be expected that they are actively maintaining options in South Africa. Although there has as yet been no large-scale exodus of whites from Namibia comparable to the stream that left Zimbabwe before and after independence, many people are making preparations for such a move, which will be far easier from Namibia to South Africa than was the case for emigrants from Zimbabwe, Mozambique, or Angola. The total lack of any restrictions on the expatriation of capital or other assets, and the close affinity between South Africans and Afrikaans- and English-speaking whites in Namibia may result in a far more rapid and complete exodus, should the balance for those inside Namibia eventually tip against staying.

However, a new class of white Namibians is also in the process of expanding. This group includes recent immigrants and expatriates, in addition to permanently settled whites who (as in Zimbabwe) have already accepted the inevitability of a change in sociopolitical structures from white to black domination, even if it results in a lowered standard of living and the loss of privileges. In the case of a large-scale white exodus, this second group might be further increased by returning white Namibians and non-Namibians interested in the development of the country, supplemented by returning black Namibians (with or without training and expertise). The large mines may be able to recruit suitable staff internationally, should the current substantial number of South Africans now working for them decline.

A third factor is the extent to which whites currently employed in the public or semipublic sectors will be needed for the future maintenance of essential services. A gradual curtailment of funds for white education (already justified in part by a decline in student numbers), or for white-only local authorities, will decrease the need for some staff.

Fourth, serious efforts to develop the black rural areas, to make land reform work in the modern agricultural sector, and to expand education and training require skilled staff, few of whom, in the short run, could be found among local blacks. At present, such new posts are not being created or filled. In the future, after the establishment of an internationally recognized independence, rural growth may be an area where external development aid could make a major contribution.

In line with the ethnic approach of the present government, the current administrative system in Namibia is both centralized—insofar as funds and final authority rest with the Ministerial Council and Windhoek, if not the Administrator General and Pretoria—and decentralized—as eleven ethnic groups are each supposed to have a government of their own (the second-tier governments, which are ethnically and not regionally defined). The same structure operates at the local-authority level, where racially differentiated bodies run submunicipalities in the towns. In the "nonwhite" governments and semistate bodies (regional development bodies, for example), whites constitute a small segment of the more senior staff and could, if necessary, be replaced relatively easily by local blacks or by other expatriates. The level of efficiency of these services is limited and standards need not decline dramatically with the departure of the top white echelon.

In the white "ethnic" administration, including the municipalities of white towns and the semistate enterprises (marketing boards, hospitals, and training institutions), the present relatively high level of efficiency is crucially dependent upon the skilled, almost exclusively white, staff. A rapid exodus of this staff would lead to a fall in standards, in many ways comparable to recent trends in Zimbabwe. It is in this area that fundamental political change would have the most far-reaching consequences, particularly since a visible drop in standards might accelerate the exodus of whites.

Although it would be necessary to consider in detail every sector and occupational category to arrive at a realistic estimate of future external manpower needs, it can be said in conclusion that between 3,000 and 5,000 skilled and experienced persons would have to be found during and after a transition to effective black government to prevent such a cumulative spiral of deterioration.

Education and Training. During the past few years, serious efforts have been made by the government to expand education in schools and to introduce a broad range of nonschool training activities. The overall trend in school education is reflected in table 3-16. These figures indicate little, however, about such problems as high drop-out rates, poorly qualified teachers, antiquated curricula, high pupil/teacher ratios, inadequate school buildings and equipment, and the differences in standards of educational services for whites and other groups. On the whole, the position of black education in Namibia differs little from that of blacks in South Africa, even though a recent decision by the Ministerial Council, following recommendations of the van Eeden Commission, will result in some redistribution of funds in favor of black education.

In the field of nonschool education, new training centers have been created—for example, the new multiracial Academy of Tertiary Education in Windhoek (which is essentially a technical college); the railway-artisan training center (which was started in Otjihase); the white-only teacher-training college (about which there have already been second thoughts and which could easily be restructured to constitute the basis for an open University of Namibia); Rössing's adult education center, and, in Ongwediva, the CDM-sponsored technical high school. Yet, as the number of black matriculants (secondary-school graduates) is so low

Table 3-16
Trends in Education, 1970-1980

	1970	1975	1976	1977	1978[a]	1979	1980
All students	133,816	182,706	190,153	203,927	214,189	224,883	240,387
Black and Bushmen	92,786	134,551	140,643	152,432	163,633	173,433	186,849
Brown	18,980	25,707	26,698	27,901	28,414	29,340	31,863
White	22,050	22,448	28,812	23,594	22,142	22,110	21,675
Primary-school pupils	123,110	166,747	170,789	181,678	189,242	198,077	212,738
Black and Bushmen	90,282	129,927	133,085	143,139	152,031	160,786	173,702
Brown	17,785	22,187	22,907	23,715	23,772	24,408	26,502
White	15,043	14,633	14,797	14,824	13,439	12,883	12,534
Secondary-school pupils	9,789	14,562	17,858	19,986	22,020	22,886	23,746
Black and Bushmen	1,943	3,654	6,517	8,388	10,605	11,609	12,301
Brown	1,195	3,520	3,791	4,186	4,455	4,659	5,103
White	6,651	7,388	7,550	7,412	6,960	6,618	6,342
Teachers	3,899	5,269	5,604	6,039	6,435	6,836	7,395
Black and Bushmen	2,042	3,142	3,473	3,829	4,265	4,596	5,066
Brown	679	890	924	977	1,003	1,039	1,123
White	1,178	1,237	1,027	1,233	1,167	1,201	1,206
Schools	607	751	792	822	888	920	965
Black and Bushmen	422	571	611	641	711	743	786
Brown	105	100	101	102	102	103	107
White	80	80	80	79	75	74	72

Source: Adapted from Africa Institute, *Bulletin*, xii/xii (1981) table 10.
[a] Walvis Bay excluded from 1978.

(only a few dozen annually in recent years), no rapid progress can be expected from any of these programs.

It is difficult to gauge what headway is being made with systematic in-service training in the civil service, by local authorities, and by other large employers. The intensiveness and scope of such efforts are still more limited than was the case in Zimbabwe during the Smith and Muzorewa governments. As in Zimbabwe, the outflow of young black exiles, and the recently broadened military service, have effectively reduced the number of blacks available for training. Table 3–17 summarizes the main elements of a rational and comprehensive educational strategy for post-independence Namibia.[12]

Housing. The sharp contrast in housing standards for white and black Namibians, and the striking differences in residential infrastructure in white and black areas, constitute a potential for considerable conflict in the future. However, there is little doubt that financial resources are at present insufficient to provide housing and infrastructural facilities of comparatively high standards to all people in the urban areas. An inevitable increase in the rate of urbanization will make the relationship between demands and available financial resources even more disproportionate.

The elements of a rational housing strategy are not difficult to list. They include opening up white towns, stimulating home-ownership at various price levels and standards, the encouragement of self-help, low-cost housing, and the maintenance of at least minimum urban infrastructure standards with public funds (allowing the private sector to supplement standards on a cost-covering basis). The difficulties center around a lack of political motivation for the dominant white municipalities to implement such a strategy. As a result, conventional standards are laid down for different residential areas, and the overall lack of funds artificially curtails the amount of housing provided at any level.

Attitudes are changing in this sphere, as can be witnessed by the new approach taken toward low-cost housing in Windhoek. It is, however, doubtful whether the current general policy will be adjusted far and fast enough, so long as the ethnocentric three-tier government structure is maintained. Nevertheless, substantial residential construction and urban infrastructural development has been undertaken during recent years, and the pace of such development is likely to accelerate under the present government.

Health and Social Welfare. The same dilemma that afflicts housing also applies to health and social-welfare services. Available funds are insufficient to provide equal standards of care to all groups in the population.

Table 3-17
Educational and Training Needs

Basic Task	Nature of Education	Institutional Framework or Process

A. Environmental change
  Modernization
  Collective motivation
	Community development	1. Preschool care and education
		2. Rural community development "Animation rurale"
		3. Township community development (Neighborhood development)

B. Functional literacy	Primary-school education Adult education	1. Primary School—rural/urban bias 2. Adult education in rural/agrarian setting 3. Urban adult education
C. Secondary basic education	Day schools Evening schools Correspondence courses	1. Centrally located private/public high schools 2. Evening classes; correspondence courses; radio programs
D. Vocational training	Special schools, Colleges, Short courses, Special programs	1. Special secondary schools/colleges; technical/commercial; agricultural 2. Teacher training colleges; seminaries 3. On-the-job training; apprenticeships 4. Special programs: clerical, administrative, commercial, health, and so forth
E. Academic training	Formal university studies Short program	1. Overseas studies 2. University of Namibia 3. Special programs
F. Leadership training	In-service training Special programs Exchange programs	Training for political, administrative, business, and community leaders

Source: Thomas, *Economic Development in Namibia: Towards Acceptable Development Strategies for Independent Namibia* (Munich, 1978).

As a result of the ethnic differentiation, the various authorities are not funded at the same per-capita levels, although a minimum amount is now being made available to each authority through a redistribution of government revenues. But, these funds are not sufficient to implement a rational policy of grassroots community health services in black areas. In addition, it has been stated explicitly that the ethnic governments should not "allow" a rapid expansion of pensioners because present funds are insufficient to cover all of the individuals who would qualify.[13]

Visible progress has been made during recent years in all of the spheres of social development that have been discussed. Yet, the diffusion from urban to rural areas is still limited, and narrowing the differences between whites and the other groups is a slow process. As a result of the constitutional entrenchment of ethnic differentiation and the system of three-tier government, blacks are convinced that race-class differences are also being entrenched. As a result, actual progress is often not recognized and political discontent persists. The maintenance of high standards for whites has, however, so far helped to prevent their rapid exodus—but at a heavy cost.

Alternative Development Strategies

Within the limited scope of this chapter it is difficult to give sufficient attention to the relative merits of alternative development strategies that might be open to a soon-to-be-independent Namibia. To combine an awareness of the status quo and a future perspective with some consideration of alternative strategies I look at three possibilities that could arise in different contexts.[14]

The first alternative is the continuation of the status quo by a DTA government. This possibility is discussed on the basis of pre-independence realities. The second alternative, a radical shift to a centralized socialist strategy, might be the result of a clearcut SWAPO victory in open elections, with the future government dominated by SWAPO's more radical leaders. The third alternative assumes a SWAPO-oriented strategy, but with moderates or pragmatists in control of policymaking. This situation could be the result of an electoral victory by moderates or could come about if the ideological fervor of the radicals were tempered in the light of economic and other realities and constraints.

Continuation of the Status Quo

Key elements of a conservative strategy include the following continuation of the three-tier ethnic structure of government, with a limited amount of income redistribution through the central government's budget; continuation—and possibly even a widening—of the disparity in development and income levels between the money sector and the subsistence sector; slow and only limited expansion of the public sector and of the interventionist role of government (although with a continuation of ad hoc controls); increasing unemployment due to rising capital/labor ratios, along with the neglect of the rural sector and restrictions on urban growth; large-scale financial, administrative, and skilled manpower dependence on South Africa; and close import, marketing, and other economic links with South Africa.

With such a development strategy, it would be unlikely that either internal black opposition or external political (and military) pressure upon the country would subside. Namibia might then evolve into a type of "siege economy" not unlike that that characterized Zimbabwe before its independence.

Aspects of such development might include skilled and semiskilled labor shortages as a result of demands by the defense forces and other security services, a steady outflow of both whites (potential recruits and older persons) and blacks (to join the so-called liberation movement), and increasing difficulty in attracting foreign (for example, South African, Zimbabwean, and overseas) skilled workers on contract. Defense and security spending would rise rapidly (not all of which would be borne by South Africa), and spending on other functions hitherto fulfilled by South Africa would also increase. Private-capital outflow, which already amounted to large sums in 1976, but declined when hopes rose for a peaceful settlement, would again escalate. Output in the modern agricultural sector would stagnate, if not decline, and little recovery would occur in fishing or industry, although turnover in the commercial sector and consumer spending would increase due to high overall spending by government, and upward trends in wage and salary levels. Potential foreign investors interested in mining and other fields would be discouraged due to international pressure and uncertainty about future developments. Disruption of economic activities in the northern, "operational" areas would increase, thus preventing any lasting success for attempts at rural development and social improvement. Open, as well as concealed, unemployment would rise (although this trend would be offset by the recruitment of soldiers from all population groups).

Taken together, these factors suggest that, in the short term, Namibia's economy runs the danger of becoming more unbalanced and more dependent upon the few major mining companies. It is in danger of stagnating even beyond the current recession caused by the drought and the mining slump. As a result, the gap between rising black expectations and the ability to meet them is likely to widen. Most of the additional revenue created by the mining sector could easily be taken up by direct and indirect increases in security spending, and, therefore, attempts at structural change and economic improvement would fail due to lack of funds. Taking a longer view, the balance resulting from the maintenance of the political status quo may gradually shift from economic gains to losses, thus reinforcing other political pressures for change. This first alternative is unstable, even though it might be maintained for several more years because of South Africa's military superiority in the region.

A Socialist Namibia

If the radical or socialist wing of SWAPO were to dominate a postindependence government and attempt to implement its principles in a rigid, noncompromising way, a totally new Namibia might be created almost overnight, although it is doubtful that this situation would be allowed to exist for long. Elements of such a strategy probably would include the following aspects, most of which have been mentioned in SWAPO-oriented political documents.

The mines and fish factories would be nationalized.

A comprehensive land-reform policy would be introduced through which absentee landowners and farmers with more than a stipulated land area would lose their land (probably without compensation). SWAPO supporters would take over virtually all senior public-sector posts currently held by whites. Economic links with South Africa would be drastically reduced.

Economic and political ties would be established with Scandinavian and eastern European, as well as nonaligned Third World countries (in addition to continued links with Western states).

Public funds would be redirected into grassroots education and health care. Widespread control of community, labor, and capital markets would be put into effect (including, for example, the regulation of maximum rents and prices and minimum wages).

The almost immediate result of the implementation of such a strategy would probably be the wholesale exodus of white skilled (and other) labor and workers' dependents. It is conceivable that only about 25,000 whites (10,000 workers) would remain in the country. The exodus would most likely include the top managerial, technical, financial, and administrative levels of the white labor force, as well as the majority of the approximately 5,600 remaining white farmers. Even a fair number of Coloured people might leave the country. With the outflow of skilled and managerial manpower (which might possibly exclude skeleton staffs for the major mines) would probably go the bulk of the remaining private capital.

It is unnecessary to pursue this alternative, since the South African government would not allow it to develop. South Africa has repeatedly and unequivocally stated that it would not tolerate an ideologically committed radical socialist government in Windhoek. Moreover, even if enough skilled persons could be recruited overseas to run the mines and keep the central government intact, overall economic activity and personal-income levels would probably shrink substantially under such an alternative strategy.

A Moderate "Social-Democratic" Namibia

Since this third alternative—which is widely regarded as the most desirable, and also the most probable—would have to evolve from a transitional stage, I will describe the main phases of such a process. Although much will depend upon the length of the transitional phase, the style of the election campaign, and the degree of civil unrest resulting from the return of refugees and exiled politicians, a few general observations can be made about the transitional process and ensuing governmental policies, in the light of structural characteristics outlined earlier, as well as postelection developments in Zimbabwe.

Economic Prospects. Big business—the multinational mining companies and other large business interests—although strongly opposed to a SWAPO government in the past, would probably accept a United Nations's supervised transition to nonethnic majority rule, even if it might result in a SWAPO-dominated government. During the transitional phase, these companies would be likely to adopt a low-key attitude, giving more material support to DTA but leaving all options open. It would be unlikely, however, that new investments of any significant size would be made during this phase. Any serious deterioration of internal stability might furthermore result in the establishment and implementation of contingency plans for evacuation and capital withdrawal. In the absence of restrictions on capital flow or migration to South Africa, and given the close interrelationship between major multinational corporations in Namibia and South Africa, such a withdrawal could be effected more easily than in present-day Zimbabwe, and it could be crippling to Namibia's economy.[15]

Even if no short-run mass exodus of whites takes place, considerably more emigration will occur, which, far sooner than was the case in Zimbabwe, could weaken the economy, particularly commercial agriculture, mining, the standard of tertiary services, and administrative efficiency. However, this emigration is also likely to happen in the alternative case where the status quo continues and the military conflict deepens.

The Economy in Transition to Independence 83

The short-run potential of the Namibian economy, which is promising but unbalanced and precarious, is likely to come under increasing strains. On the assumption that SWAPO's moderate leaders will dominate policymaking, the party might, however, feel restrained in much of their reform programs to avoid further economic decline. Yet, an important difference between the Zimbabwean and Namibian situations becomes apparent: Zimbabwe could hope for at least some economic momentum as a result of the end of sanctions; the very opposite is likely to happen to Namibia, which never experienced sanctions. Some dampening effects are bound to result from independence and a loosening of ties with South Africa. The positive effects of structural reforms and possible benefits of greater autonomy from South Africa would only become significant in the long run.

The very great economic interdependence of Namibia and South Africa will give the latter much influence in the transitional phase that could be used to press for moderation but could also be used to disrupt the Namibian economy, thus virtually blocking chances for a peaceful transition to independence. In the light of South Africa's long-run interest in a stable subregion, however, the latter alternative is less likely. Yet, the preconditions for economic stability are more precarious for Namibia than they were for Zimbabwe—and even for Zimbabwe recent history has illustrated dramatically the delicate mix of disrupting and stabilizing forces at work in its transitional and postindependence phases. In the light of the relatively precarious situation of the Namibian economy, the difficult task of political stabilization facing an independent Namibia, the medium-term prospects for its economy are far less promising than is sometimes assumed because of the prominence of certain minerals and past development.

Return of the Refugees. The task of reintegrating refugees and exiles will arise at an early stage of independence. Its magnitude may be less severe in Namibia than it was in Zimbabwe, although past estimates of 5,000 to 10,000 people may fall far short of the real number. If SWAPO's military force is estimated at about 10,000 it would represent a larger proportion of the total population than the Zimbabwe African Liberation Army (ZANLA)–Zimbabwe Independent Peoples' Revolutionary Army (ZIPRA) forces constituted in Zimbabwe. In addition, if independence is preceded by more intensive military action in northern Ovambo, the number of soldiers and civilians eventually returning from Angola, Zambia, and Botswana might surpass 40,000. This number would, nevertheless, be relatively small compared to the magnitude of refugee movements in other parts of Africa. As the movements are concentrated in northern and northwestern Namibia, the destabilizing effect of the returning refugees on the so-called modern sector around Windhoek might (at least initially) be less severe than those resulting from early postindependence migraton around Harare (Salisbury) in Zimbabwe.

Namibiazation and the Future Presence of Whites. Most of the discriminatory practices still existing today will, already have disappeared by independence, as was the case in Zimbabwe. But, after independence, a strategy of reverse discrimination, in the form of a mixture of affirmative action and "Namibiazation" will probably be pursued by the new government.

Combined with the rise of African nationalist and African socialist rhetoric, this process could lead to considerable estrangement between blacks and whites inside Namibia. In contrast to Zimbabwe, the bulk of Namibia's present white population may find it very hard to accept such changes, particularly if they are not limited to equal opportunities and if they become effective in Windhoek, the politically conservative, white-controlled capital city of colonial Namibia. Together with other factors—such as the loss of a direct political-power base, fear of the effects of political instability, the consequences of land reform, and a decline in real living standards—these changes may result in a significant additional outflow of whites.

The goal of maintaining existing standards of services, although not likely to be as central as it is to the current government, will probably remain important for a moderate administration. Its achievement, however, will be far less motivated by the desire to encourage the continued presence of the South Africa-rooted whites currently domiciled in the country. The relatively small total population, the key role played by a few multinational corporations, the relatively large size of the German-speaking (non-South Africa-rooted) population group, and the inherent attractiveness of Namibia as a developing black African country, may combine to make the supply of key skilled and managerial staff less problematic than is often suggested.

Implementing a New Development Strategy. In the medium term, the design, acceptance, and implementation of a new development strategy will be the most important factor shaping the economy. Policy papers prepared by or for SWAPO, recent developments in Zimbabwe and other African countries, and responses to my own publication about acceptable development strategies for independent Namibia, indicate that the following aspects will play a key role.[16]

Questions must be resolved concerning the ownership of agricultural land in the so-called white area, the utilization of land in the tribal areas, and property ownership in urban areas. The latter may be the easiest problem to resolve (although not necessarily in a way that will be acceptable to many whites) by the total elimination of all restrictions on property ownership, possibly combined with some controls on property prices and expatriate property ownership. In the tribal areas, a pattern of communal-land ownership will probably be encouraged, combined with cooperative farming enterprises. The most sensitive aspect is the reform of land ownership in the commercial-agricultural sector. As in Zimbabwe, this problem could be eased by the voluntary emigration of some of the 5,600 white farmers and by more effective control of absentee land ownership. After independence enough of this land might be available to satisfy the demand of black farmers (assisted by a nonracial Namibian land and agricultural bank). The bigger problem will be to prevent overfragmentation of the land and to find competent persons to manage the ranch-type farms, bearing in mind the delicate ecological balance that exists in most parts of Namibia.[17]

As in Zimbabwe, it can be expected that a new government will place major emphasis on steps to improve peasant agriculture in the more fertile northern areas. This direction might be reflected in a major shift in the allocation of public funds, the attraction of foreign aid, and the establishment of training facilities. At best, however, success will be slow.

As in other African countries, the problem of unemployment will be one of the biggest challenges facing the new government. With the present estimated rate of un(der)employment already put at 25 percent of the labor force; a likelihood of at least an interim stagnation in mining, commercial agriculture, and the services sector; and with increasing difficulty in stemming rural-urban migration, open unemployment is likely to become a major threat to Namibia's postindependence political stability. As short-run solutions, some of the following steps are possible: government-mandated increases (of 10 to 20 percent) in paid employment for larger enterprises; the encouragement of squatter farming on commercial-sector farms; the establishment of an ad hoc (paramilitary) job corps or rural-brigade scheme; a relatively slow dismantling of military forces; and the establishment of local processing facilities for food products (import substitution).

In light of the strong feelings held by SWAPO about the past and present role of major mining concerns, it is likely that a new government will insist on a renegotiation of present production, tax, and export arrangements and, probably, the transfer of some share of ownership to a government-controlled mining corporation. But, because of the recent slump in mineral export prices and the gloomy prospects for future world uranium demand, and in order not to discourage foreign investment in prospecting and other new mining activities, these steps are likely to be moderate and pragmatic.

As in Zimbabwe, a new broad-based government will be under considerable pressure to expand spending for education, training, health services, housing, and other aspects of community development for its black electorate. In general, the emphasis will probably fall on satisfying basic needs, in line with much modern development thinking. This attitude may lead to increased taxes on the mining sector and to a reduction in public-sector funds available for such facilities for the higher income groups.

In SWAPO's rhetoric about the current capitalist economic system, much emphasis is placed on existing disparities in racial, regional, and occupational incomes, which would suggest by implication that after independence drastic steps will be taken to readjust this pattern. As the experience of Zimbabwe, Zambia, and Kenya shows, however, practical considerations may place severe limitations on doing so.

Since Namibia has been in the international limelight for a considerable time, much attention has already been given to an independent, and more-or-less SWAPO-oriented, assessment of Namibia's foreign-aid requirements and the possible role of international development agencies in designing and/or implementing a realistic development strategy. Should a future government maintain its links with Western democratic governments (which is highly likely), countries like West Germany, Britain, Finland, Norway, France, and the United States, as well as church organizations within these countries, are likely to play a significant role. Research undertaken during the past four years by a German aid institute could be indicative of the direction of such assistance and influence. Although the postindependence experience of Zimbabwe suggests the need for caution in establishing the dimension of foreign-aid commitments, Namibia might be in an advantageous position, particularly if the transition is characterized by a large exodus of whites to South Africa. Put differently, prospects for substantial, transitional foreign assistance in the form of manpower, training, and loans, combined with the export and revenue potential of the mining sector, might make a postindependence government of Namibia less dependent on South Africa and therefore less cautious in some of its structural reforms (for example, breaking away from the Rand Monetary Area and the Customs Agreement).[18]

Future relations with South Africa will undoubtedly constitute one of the most difficult aspects of an independent Namibia's development strategy. Pragmatic considerations would suggest a balance between greater assertion of national interests and the continuation of advantageous economic ties. Whether this would (and should) include a rapid move away from the Rand Monetary Area, the Customs Agreement, or from the almost completely integrated physical infrastructure facilities cannot be determined without knowing more certainly about other characteristics of the future relations between the two countries. A moderate SWAPO government will be fully aware of the potentially crippling hold that South Africa has on Namibia's economy, given South Africa's sovereignty over Walvis Bay and the control of most of the other economic sectors by South African firms or interests.[19]

In conclusion, it is reasonable to expect that a moderate SWAPO-oriented government will display a high degree of pragmatism in its new development strategy—much in line with the recent experience of many black African countries—but that internal political pressures and a declining direct dependence on South Africa may make the government less hesitant to undertake far-reaching structural reforms than might be expected in the light of Zimbabwe's early postindependence performance. Actual progress in advancing real living standards and implementing comprehensive rural development in the more densely populated areas may, nevertheless, be slow and dependent largely upon the expansion of mining exports, the training and development of local manpower, and the achievement of political stability.

Conclusion: Can the Impasse be Broken?

For the critical observer of Namibia's lingering transition process from virtual integration within South Africa to internationally recognized independence, this descriptive overview and cautious prognosis may seem incomplete even if the complementary nature of Kate Jowell's chapter is taken into account. Three further questions call for tentative answers. First, how has the bulk of the Namibian population been affected by socioeconomic developments during the pat decade? Second, how likely is a final breakthrough in the impasse involving South Africa and the DTA on the one side, SWAPO and its Third World supporters on the other side, and the Western negotiators in the middle? If a resolution is not likely, how will this affect socioeconomic developments in the country? Third, is it realistic to expect a moderate, sociodemocratic outcome from the transition to independence if SWAPO or a SWAPO/center-left coalition wins the elections? If not, what can be expected to happen to Namibia's economy over the next decade or two?

This chapter has presented an evolutionary perspective on future developments, and these questions call for a nonevolutionary, conflict-centered perspective. In the following, some consideration is given to this perspective, without thereby suggesting an inevitable discontinuity between the two approaches.

The question of how the bulk of Namibia's rural-based black population has been affected by socioeconomic developments during the past decade has been considered far too seldom in discussions about the country's overall economic performance. About 80 percent of the total population is settled far away from any of the few urban centers, and about their social and material development few reliable indicators exist. We know that the educational system has expanded (in a quantitative, if not always a qualitative, sense); health facilities have improved in the larger villages, which has indirectly benefited the nearby rural settlements; and urban workers have probably transferred increasing amounts of money to their dependents in the rural areas. Improved transport services and an increase in motor-vehicle ownership have also brought many of the rural areas into closer contact with urban centers.

Yet, for the mass of the rural population, especially in the northern areas and in the more remote regions in central and southern Namibia, subsistence agriculture and a living standard far below scientifically calculated household subsistence levels are still the rule. Most of the development efforts of the last decade have not reached the grassroots level in the rural areas or led to continued and clearly visible material progress among the rural population. The whole concept of integrated rural development is still very much in its infancy and the preconditions for success are largely missing at this stage.

The situation in the rural areas is further aggravated by two facts. First, rural dwellers are aware that material standards are improving in the urban areas and that, in addition to the whites, a new black urban elite is benefiting disproportionately from development efforts. Relative deprivation of rural communities has probably increased during the past decade. Second, the rural population has had to bear the brunt of the war in the "operational areas," which has involved the loss of lives on a large scale, the absence of husbands and sons who went north and therefore could no longer support their families, frequent destruction of huts and other property in war-related activities, and often the loss or damage of crops and infrastructural facilities. In some cases, the rural population has been drawn together in so-called protected villages, which has resulted in a temporary loss of subsistence earnings and a sudden separation from the rural environment without replacement by some superior urban environment.

Bearing in mind the regional distribution of Namibia's population and the low rate of urbanization, it may not be far fetched to postulate that the majority of the population has regarded developments during the past decade as socioeconomically retrogressive, and that they therefore are looking forward to a change of government as a precondition for peace and for more lasting improvements in their living standard.

The second question relates to the key issue underlying all recent speculation about Namibia's transition to independence: Will South Africa allow internationally supervised elections to take place in Namibia, and will it recognize whatever government gets elected? For more than five years the five Western powers have been negotiating for such a solution, but, whenever a breakthrough is imminent, new obstacles arise and further negotiations become necessary. Even after the successful conclusion of phase one of the most recent Western round of initiatives, so many issues remain unresolved that few informed observers believe that independence is closer than the usual "two to three years" from the present.

What are the consequences of this stalemate for the country's socioeconomic development? South Africa will probably continue to give substantial financial assistance to Namibia, even though this aid may be insufficient to broaden the development base. The benefits will continue to accrue largely to urban areas and to the relatively small new elite. In the rural areas, progress will continue with respect to education, improvement of the infrastructure, and some modernization of agricultural techniques. Yet, in line with many development trends in other parts of black Africa, the rural-urban gap will widen further, and urban dwellers will try their best to keep rural-urban migration under control. In addition, war activities are likely to continue to take a heavier toll from rural than urban communities.

The longer the present stalemate continues, the less likely it is that eventual elections will bring forward a moderate, sociodemocratically oriented government. Not only will those potential black coalition partners for a SWAPO government who are at present still inside the country be discredited (as members of the new internal elite) but continuation of the war will deepen animosities, as has been shown in Zimbabwe. Once we take into account such a gradual trend toward radicalization, it becomes difficult to keep predicting a moderate socioeconomic strategy after the eventual takeover by a popularly elected government.

Notes

1. H. Brandt, et al., *Perspectives on Independent Development in Southern Africa: The Case of Zimbabwe and Namibia* (Berlin, 1980); Reginald H. Green, *Manpower Estimates and Development Implications for Namibia* (Lusaka, 1978); Green, "The Unforgiving Land—Basis for a Post-Liberation Programme in Namibia," *IDS Bulletin,* XI (1980), 70–76; *idem,* "Transition to What? Some Issues of Freedom and Necessity in Namibia," *Development and Change,* XI (1980), 419–454; E. Leistner, et al., *Namibia/SWA Prospectus* (Pretoria, 1980); Roger Murray, *The Mineral Industry of Namibia: Perspectives for Independence* (London, 1979); Sue Collett, "The Economy of South-West Africa: Current Con-

ditions and Some Future Prospects," unpub. ms. (Johannesburg, 1978); idem, "The Human Factor in the Economic Development of Namibia," *Optima*, XXVIII (1980), 191–219; Karsten E.B. von Kleist, *Förderung des Tourismus als Beitrag zur gesamtwirtschaftlichen und gesamtgesellschaftlichen Entwicklung von SWA/Namibia* (Oxford, 1980).

2. On the language issue, see United Nations Institute for Namibia (UNIN), *Toward a Language Policy for Namibia* (Lusaka, 1981).

3. A.M. Mramba, "Possibilities for the Future Development of Livestock Ranching in an Independent Namibia," unpub. M.A. diss. (University of Sussex, 1977); S. Mshonga, *Agrarian Reform Options for an Independent Namibia* (Lusaka, 1979); Brandt, "Perspektiven der Agrarentwicklung eines Unabhängigen Namibia," *Afrika Spectrum*, XIV (1979), 203–217; C. Nixon, *Land Use and Development in Namibia* (Lusaka, 1978); N.K. Duggal (ed.), *Constitutional Options for Namibia: A Historical Perspective* (Lusaka, 1979).

4. Murray, *The Mineral Industry;* W. Gocht, *Namibia: Sektorstudie Bergbau* (Berlin, 1979).

5. See also W. Schneider-Barthold, *Namibia: Sektor-studie Industrie* (Berlin, 1979).

6. Economic Advisory Committee, *The Economy of SWA/Namibia: Problems, Future Prospects and Required Policy Measures* (Windhoek, 1978/1980), 31.

7. Kleist, *Förderung des Tourismus*.

8. Deloitte, Haskins, and Sells, Ltd., *Taxation in South-West Africa/Namibia* (Windhoek, 1982).

9. See F.B. Gebhardt, "The Socio-economic Status of Farm Labourers in Namibia," *South African Labour Bulletin*, IV (1978), 145–173, about farm labor. On labor relations, see Barbara Rogers, *White Wealth and Black Poverty: American Investments in Southern Africa* (London, 1980), 170–216; K. Gottschalk, "South African Labour Policy in Namibia, 1915–1975," *South Africa Labour Bulletin*, IV (1978), 75–106.

10. On labor and employment, see Neville Rubin, *Labour and Discrimination in Namibia* (Geneva, 1977); Robert J. Gordon, *Mines, Masters and Migrants: Life in a Namibian Mine Compound* (Johannesburg, 1977); Gillian and Suzanne Cronje, *The Workers of Namibia* (London, 1979); Charles T. Truebody, *Labour Relations in South-West Africa—A First Assessment* (Windhoek, 1982). On property rights, see M. O'Callaghan, *Namibia: The Effects of Apartheid on Culture and Education* (Paris, 1977).

11. Green, "Manpower Estimates"; UNIN, *Toward Manpower Development for Namibia* (Lusaka, 1977); Thomas, *Namibia: Beschäftingungsstruktur und Arbeitskräftebedarf* (Berlin, 1979).

The Economy in Transition to Independence

12. On the possibility of an open University of Namibia, see C.M. Rogerson, "A Future 'University of Namibia'? The Role of the U.N. Institute for Namibia," *Journal of Modern African Studies,* XVIII (1980), 675–683. In addition to table 3–17, see also Gudrun Lachenmann, *Namibia: Sektorstudie Bildungswesen* (Berlin, 1979); Henning Melber, *Schule und Kolonialismus: Das Formale Erziehungswesen Namibias* (Hamburg, 1979).

13. See Kenneth G. Abrahams, "Memorandum presented to the Commission of Inquiry into Health Services in SWA," unpub. ms. (Windhoek, 1981); Lachenmann, *Namibia: Sektorstudie Gesundheitwesen* (Berlin, 1979); idem, "Die 'getrennte Entwicklung' der Gesundheit in Namibia," *Afrika-Spectrum,* LXXX (1980), 147–162.

14. See Green, *Namibia: A Political Economy Survey* (Sussex, 1979).

15. See Namibia Support Committee, *Foreign Companies in Namibia: A Short List of Western Firms* (London, 1980).

16. Thomas, *Economic Development in Namibia: Towards Acceptable Strategies for Independent Namibia* (Munich, 1978).

17. See Nixon, *Land Use and Development;* Mshonga, *Toward Agrarian Reform: Policy Options for Namibia* (Lusaka, 1979).

18. Brandt et al., *Perspectives on Independent Development;* Samuel C. Adams, *Zimbabwe and Namibia: Anticipation of Economic and Humanitarian Needs* (Washington, D.C., 1977); United States Agency for International Development, *Development Needs and Opportunities for Cooperation in Southern Africa—Annexure A* (Washington, D.C., 1979); United Nations Council for Namibia, *Pre-Independence Period Project Proposals for the Nationhood Programme for Namibia* (New York, 1978), 2v.; United Nations Food and Agriculture Organization, *Namibia: Prospects for Future Development* (Rome, 1977). On the direction of Western assistance, see Schneider-Barthold, *Namibia's Economic Potential and Existing Economic Ties with the Republic of South Africa* (Berlin, 1977); Brandt et al., *Perspectives on Independent Development.*

19. See Wolfgang Zehender, "Aussenwirtschaftliche Perspektiven fur ein unabhangiges Namibia," *Afrika Spectrum,* LXXX (1980), 135–147; Green, *Namibia: A Political Economy Survey.*

4 Economic Priorities for an Independent Namibia

Kate Jowell

Anyone bold enough to catalogue the economic priorities for an independent Namibia has to start by making several risky assumptions. The first is about the political character of the postindependence government. If it is SWAPO dominated, as is believed to be likely almost everywhere except in South Africa, it is equally likely that the country's financial lifelines to Pretoria will be cut, leaving it with a substantial budget deficit.

Opinions diverge over the territory's economic future. As Thomas points out in this book, some experts say that the country is poor in resources, economically unstable, and hampered by nature. Others believe that it is one of the best-endowed African countries relative to its population. Certainly, its level of literacy, its school population, and its road and rail infrastructure are substantially better than in many other African countries, as Thomas shows. However, the fragility of Namibia's economy in the immediate postindependence period is unarguable. This fact leads to a second important assumption: the leaders of the newly independent state will be conscious of that fragility and of the limitations that it should place on a radical restructuring of the economy in the short term.

Given these assumptions, the overall economic consequences are reasonably obvious. What will be required in the initial stages of a takeover of the government and purse strings in Namibia is stability and the creation of a framework for the second stage, when an orderly and possibly more fair development of the territory can take place. Economic policy should be directed toward these conservative ends.

This conclusion was the consensus of the conference study group that met at Ditchley late in 1981 to discuss Namibia's economic priorities. It was hardly surprising that this group would take such a pragmatic view, given the strong concentration of economists and businessmen. It is also not surprising that this conservative bias came under attack. Some participants empahsized different priorities, or at least different policy choices within those priorities, for reasons of political conviction or expediency.

The pragmatic view dictated six priorities for Namibia, if stability and a basically sound economic framework were to be established. The first, and most obvious, of these priorities is to find ways to stabilize the country's manpower resources, which are concentrated in mining, the civil service, agriculture, and secondary industry and commerce. The new government would want to avoid, or at best minimize, an exodus of frightened or disenchanted whites, who represent the bulk of the skilled workforce.

The extent of the exodus will depend on what kind of transition is made to independence and on what reassurances are given in the immediate postindependence period. This transition is particularly important with respect to the civil service, for the prospects for instability are greater there than in other sectors of the economy, due to its domination by Afrikaans-speaking whites who are loyal to South Africa.

Elsewhere in Africa, the presence of a legitimate colonial government in the transition period has made it possible to smooth the changeover—if only to the limited extent of making clear how the civil service would be run in future, what would happen to pensions, whether gratuities would be paid, and so forth. Ideally, the arrangements for transition should be made more comprehensively, as was the case in Kenya, for example, where a task force began preparing for the changeover a year before. Such help would be available to Namibia now, except for the injunction from the International Court that stops the Contact Group from dealing with the South African administration in any way that would be tantamount to legalizing its "illegal" rule of the territory. The Namibia Institute (in Zambia) has been training prospective civil servants, but they are few and lack practical experience.

In agriculture, the confidence of the largely white commercial farmers must be maintained, not simply because of the value of agricultural production as an export but also to secure the jobs of the 44,000 blacks who are engaged in this sector. The small but vital group of veterinary surgeons who service this industry need particularly careful attention, as their departure could cause a collapse of the controls on foot-and-mouth disease.

A greater degree of stability might exist in the commercial sector, where German-speaking whites predominate—some say because they have been more receptive to political change in the past few years and more open to the advent of a black government. If there is an exodus of technicians from the mining industry, its manpower needs could be met in the short term, albeit at some cost, by non-South African expatriates, although this solution is not adequate in the long run.

Theoretically, Namibia has a sufficient indigenous population to fill any manpower needs. However, it is poorly educated and lacks training. One of the tragedies of this pre-independence period is that, although money and support are available from international educational and training institutions and agencies, the "illegality" of the current administration prevents it from being offered. A substantial amount of money and effort is being put into training and education by the multinational corporations already in Namibia, but their efforts are not sufficient to tackle the whole problem.

How well manpower is stabilized has a bearing on the second economic priority: the need to ensure the continuity and development of production in the three main areas of the economy—mining, agriculture, and secondary industry and commerce.

In the short term, the mining sector needs only a continuing and growing supply of skilled people—artisans and middle managers—to maintain its existing level of production. But mining, and the development of new mines, has a long, high-risk horizon. Continuity of mining operations and the development of known mineral resources depend more on the outlook for commodity prices than on any other factor. Nevertheless, the ultimate feasibility of new mines, and the continued production of those currently established, would be heavily influenced by the political and economic policies that a new government would pursue. What will the new administration's approach be to taxes and investment incentives? Will profits continue to be repatriable? Will the government want a share of ownership? What social issues face mining companies? A key issue will probably be wage levels.

There has been talk in some quarters in Namibia of a national minimum wage and veiled references by SWAPO sources to the need for the mines to make more of a contribution to development. By its nature, the mining industry does not scare easily but, for the multinational corporations that dominate it, there have been many precedents and experiences to ponder.

At present, the continuity of the farming sector is not an issue. Because of the crippling drought in the territory, there is no meat industry to speak of, and the once promising game-farming business has withered. A widespread exodus of farmers has already taken place, many leaving Namibia for the suburbs of Cape Town and its dormitory town, Somerset West, in South Africa.

Some experts believe that a large number of the territory's farms would benefit from lying fallow for a period of years because of the extensive overfarming that has recently taken place. However, this suggestion presupposes that the vacuum left by white commercial farmers will not be filed by black peasants hungry for acreage, who may further damage the land.

Another serious consideration for this industry is its dependence on South Africa, both as a market and for distribution. Although the new abattoir at Gobabis is reported to be able to process nearly three-quarters of Namibia's stock under normal conditions, it is unlikely that the industry could reproduce the marketing structure and distribution channels that it presently enjoys in South Africa. There is talk of building a road linking Gobabis and Gaberone (through Jwaneng) that would expedite the export of cattle from Namibia through Botswana, but a fuller use of the facilities at Gobabis is academic at this point.

Land reform (usually a priority of new national governments) and agricultural development are two related issues. Good potential for reform exists in the northern areas, where current forms of land tenure militate against agricultural productivity. Ending hostilities in the north would allow for a rapproachement with Angola, opening up the possibility of a market for agricultural products in that country and maybe even for food that has been processed in simple ways. The processing of agricultural products is generally thought to be one of the best, and also one of the few, options available for the development of secondary industry in the country. Such development has proceeded slowly, and will remain limited by the availability of manpower and skills.

Continuity is very important, too, in secondary industry and commerce. This sector is not significant in terms of gross national product (GNP), but it now employs some 16 percent of the workforce—15 percent of the blacks and 20 percent of the whites. Small entrepreneurs everywhere have a low risk threshold, and deterioration in the nation's shopping and service sectors would produce a very quick and visible effect on morale in the community—second only to the drop in morale and security that comes when local authorities are unable to keep the trash barrels emptied or maintain the streets in the Western style to which most "colonial" whites are accustomed. The substantial participation of Namibians of German extraction in the secondary sector could provide a buffer against panicked disinvolvement, but this is only conjecture.

A third issue that must exercise the mind of a new Namibian government is South Africa's domination of the transport and communication structure within the territory. In any nonviolent transfer of power, South Africa would probably continue to run the system and assist in the transition phase. However, if the transition were not peaceful, or not one that found favor with the South African government, or if, as some people suggest, South Africa has an interest in destabilizing the black states on its own borders, then the situation could be considerably more problematic. The difficulties experienced by Zimbabwe in 1981 over the shortage of rolling stock for its railways would provide a healthy object lesson to a new Namibian government on the extent of its dependence on Pretoria's goodwill.

Whatever the kind of transition, some key questions will arise. The first is whether Namibia is moving fast enough to detach itself from South

Africa. The post office and the railways are training Namibians to take over key posts. The railway already operates under its own territorial manager, but it is not clear whether the shift to autonomy is being planned comprehensively or being executed with sufficient purpose.

The South African government is believed to be considering a report on various ways to transfer some of the transport infrastructure to Namibian management. How greatly these alternatives hinge on the settlement negotiations is not clear. The issue of who will pay has also to be determined. How high are Namibia's transport needs on the agenda of institutions such as the World Bank? Are potential foreign-aid partners aware that South Africa's control of transport is a tactical weapon that could be used against Namibia? Will foreign aid be coordinated so as to take the sting out of this weapon?

Presumably, these questions are being addressed by SWAPO's policymakers. Namibia could probably join with other black states that have coordinated their infrastructural development efforts. Angola, Botswana, Lesotho, Malawi, Mozambique, Swaziland, Tanzania, Zimbabwe, and Zambia are members of the Southern African Transport and Communication Commission, which has a series of development plans. The Southern African Development Coordination Conference (SADCC), formed by Prime Minister Robert Mugabe of Zimbabwe and other leaders, is reputed to have no less than nine hundred transport and commercial projects on its drawing boards, but it has only recently begun to raise the R 2 billion that it needs to finance its plans.

The fourth economic priority is the question of Namibia's dependence on South Africa for the financing of its public debt. As Thomas shows, South Africa contributes a handsome R 200 to R 300 million to the Namibian regular budget, around one-third of the total. Closer inspection reveals that large sums currently being spent might possibly disappear at independence. What, for example, is likely to happen to the amazing total of R 42 million spent on "constitutional development" in 1981/1982? New sources of revenue do not immediately present themselves, and existing ones are currently depressed. One such, the uranium industry, is not expected to contribute a great deal to the national exchequer in the near future because of the poor state of the uranium market. Diamond sales are also severely down and, with stockpiles high, no early recovery can be predicted.

The consensus at the Ditchley conference was that much of the padding in the current Namibian budget could be stripped away and that, under less depressed conditions, the territory could live largely within its means, meeting any deficits with conventional development aid. This assertion presupposes, however, a peaceful transition period without loss of confidence, either internally or externally, in the territory's future, and a strong and stable transition government that can maintain a balance between pragmatism and the need to satisfy an electorate with high expectations.

Much has been made of Namibia's dependence on South Africa, but it could also be argued that South Africa's monetary authorities will view the territory's departure from the republic's books with regret. As a major exporter, Namibia has had a positive balance of payments for some years, which has helped South Africa, with its tendency to run deficits on its own balance of payments.

This fact leads to the fifth of the economic priorities to which the new government must address itself: a set of questions on monetary and other policy issues. Should Namibia, for example, detach itself from the Rand Monetary Area and establish a separate currency and separate monetary authority? Unlike South Africa, Namibia has limited exchange controls. Should it hinder the movement of currency in the immediate postindependence period, or will such a restriction lead to a higher degree of panic and insecurity and a greater exodus of white skills? Is there value in retaining a customs union with South Africa?

These are complicated questions that cannot be properly answered without detailed study and investigation. Superficially, there appears to be no benefit in introducing exchange control regulations, which would probably undermine confidence and so be counterproductive. There also seems to be no rational reason why Namibia should not retain the customs union with South Africa that currently brings in about R 250 million annually. There is a distinct value in such an arrangement, as the Botswanans have realized. It appears perfectly possible, given the Botswanan experience, for an anti-Pretoria government to retain this link and also maintain credibility with its allies farther north.

Political credibility in Africa is an exceptionally sensitive issue. This became clear when the group considered its sixth and final economic priority—the value of economic cooperation of a broader kind, which the Namibian government must of necessity seek. Ultimately, there are only four possible economic partners for Namibia, although two, at least, are unlikely. Namibia could become part of the Lomé Convention, but admission would be a slow process. Namibia would also be entitled to ask for membership in the British Commonwealth, but the value of this tie would be limited largely to technical aid.

The third possibility is SADCC, which was formed as a counterpoint to South Africa's Constellation of States—the fourth possible partner. As yet, SADCC is still only a policy coordinating group, and very few of its ideas have been implemented. However, Namibia could explore possible links with SADCC in a low-key manner that would not damage any bargaining power that it might have for extracting a direct subsidy from South Africa, should such an arrangement prove politically and economically expedient.

South Africa would welcome a new recruit into the Constellation of States, its much publicized attempt to draw its neighbors into economic cooperation. Thus far, the Constellation consists in theory only of Malawi and South Africa's own "independent" states. But it would not be easy for Namibia to forge this link, regardless of how valuable it might be, and regardless of the eventual political character of the postindependence government. The political pressures against such a tie would be too severe.

The prospects for any significant economic cooperation and support for Namibia from its neighbors are thus meager. Although U.S. diplomats may be proud that Zimbabwe's first bilateral-aid agreement was signed within twelve hours of the removal of the Union Jack, the lack of continuing international support for Zimbabwe must give the SWAPO policymakers pause. And someone first has to pay for the proposed United Nations peacekeeping force. Three years ago, the United States's projected share of the cost of such a force was estimated at around $300 million—not including the expense of its transport to Namibia.

The picture painted by the Ditchley study group on economic priorities was one of fragility. The primary need was seen to be for conservative holding actions in several important areas and a cautious exploration of options in others. But the group ultimately only produced a textbook exercise in pragmatism. Namibia, in the event, is likely to be overtaken by all of the classic problems experienced by new governments in underdeveloped countries. As in the rest of Africa, Namibia's distribution of wealth, of skills, and, therefore, of opportunity, is limited. It relies partly on migrant labor in its developed sector and has problems of poor agricultural productivity and underemployment in the rural sector. It somehow has to marry a traditional economy with a money economy and deal with the ideological challenges of African socialism.

In the long term, Namibia's prospects will depend on how well it handles the policy choices or trade-offs that arise out of its problems: whether to maintain modest levels of government expenditure or meet raised expectations, to preserve achieved standards for certain people or raise standards for others, to devote revenue to capital formation or to current consumption, and so on.

There is no shortage of lessons to be learned from the experience of Namibia's neighbors and predecessors in the painful process of transition to self-rule. Thanks to South Africa's intransigence, Namibia will be the last African colonial territory to achieve independence. If nothing else, it will have had the greatest opportunity to learn.

5

SWAPO and the Postindependence Era

Stanley Uys

Namibia is one of eight southern African countries that are economically dependent in a significant degree on the Republic of South Africa. It is the most dependent, because, for more than sixty years, it has been administered by South Africa virtually as a fifth province. Its economy is integrated into South Africa's in a measure unparalleled elsewhere in southern Africa. Any Namibian government, and particularly a SWAPO government, would find its decision-making independence severely checked by its economic dependence. Painful realities would steer it along a pragmatic course. However, the long period of occupation has engendered animosities toward South Africa among the indigenous inhabitants that would militate against pragmatism.

Black Africa is familiar with economic constraints on political decision making, but its colonial masters were thousands of miles away in Western Europe; in southern Africa, the contemporary metropolitan power is white South Africa, which has a vested political interest not only in maintaining the existing economic dependence but in extending and consolidating it. This fact brought Angola, Botswana, Lesotho, Malawi, Mozambique, Swaziland, Tanzania, Zambia, and Zimbabwe together in SADCC (Southern African Development Coordination Conference), with the aim of reducing their dependence on South Africa. Namibia, under SWAPO, would join SADCC, because they would share common aims.

> SADCC is realistic about the problem that it faces: SWAPO's present political bent indicates that in the medium and long term the dependency problem both with respect to RSA and European and US based multinationals will come to the fore. In the case of RSA much will depend on that country's willingness to concede majority rule in Namibia and on its responses in the early period after independence. The extent to which at present consumer goods, capital goods, important industrial inputs and technical expertise are supplied from RSA would make it possible for that country to strike crippling blows to the Namibian economy. If there is not to be immediate chaos there will need to be no more than a gradual switch of connections away from RSA. The achievement of Namibian sovereignty over Walvis Bay, the linking of

Namibia's rail system to Botswana's and better access to the Angolan industrial centre will be vital issues during this slow transition.[1]

In most Western eyes, "pragmatism" is a common-sense option, but a SWAPO government would have a different perception. SWAPO's commitment is to socialism, and pragmatism in this context means putting socialism on the shelf. SWAPO would see this constraint as an impairment of its integrity as a government, which would give rise to tensions within its ranks as the more ideologically fervent members demanded an acceleration of the pace of change. SWAPO would want Namibia to become part of the African ethos—to join the Organization of African Unity (OAU) and SADCC. South Africa would seek to promote its rival groups, the Constellation of States of Southern Africa, which SADCC sees as "simply apartheid as foreign policy." As SADCC said at its Lusaka conference:

> In the interest of the people of our countries, it is necessary to liberate our economies from their dependence on the Republic of South Africa, to overcome the imposed economic fragmentation and to co-ordinate our efforts towards regional and national economic development. This will be as great for Namibia as it is for all the independent States of the region.[2]

Westerners need to understand SWAPO's aspirations, however mistaken they believe these to be. Pragmatism is not an easy option for a SWAPO government. A pragmatic policy after independence would raise a debate in the organization on the meaning of that independence. SWAPO knows exactly what economic dependence on South Africa entails: it has considered that question for years, and has set out its conclusions both in its 1976 Political Program and, more recently; in *To Be Born A Nation: The Liberation Struggle for Namibia*.[3]

In the Political Program, which its Central Committee adopted in 1976, SWAPO pledged itself to a socialist transformation of Namibian society, and, in accordance with the principles laid down in the program, it has already begun to prepare "contingency plans for economic and social reconstruction so that the Namibian people will have before them a strategy for achieving a self-reliant and liberated society when victory is finally won."[4]

But the dilemma would still be there: on the one hand would be the familiar crisis of expectations among SWAPO's followers; on the other, the realities of dependence. A psychological crisis of trust would arise, too. Although SWAPO supporters would look to their government for tangible evidence that independence had been achieved, South Africa and the transnationals would expect contrary reassurances to allay their fears of radical change.

SWAPO and the Postindependence Era

A SWAPO government, too, would be deeply distrustful of South Africa's motives. Recently, the leaders of Angola, Zambia, Zimbabwe, Mozambique, Botswana, and Lesotho have each accused Pretoria of trying to destabilize their governments. SWAPO would ask itself why Namibia should be an exception. In an interview Prime Minister Robert Mugabe of Zimbabwe said: "Right across the length and breadth of our Southern African sub-continent, from the Atlantic Ocean to the Indian Ocean, South Africa is trying to influence the direction of events, both by military methods and by trying to destabilise the economies of the countries of the region."[5]

SWAPO has also seen, how, through the constellation idea, Pretoria has sought (unsuccessfully so far) to institutionalize its neighbors' dependence within a political-economic framework. Opposition also exists from right-wing whites in South Africa and Namibia to Namibian independence—a factor that will make it necessary for Pretoria, both before and after independence, to be seen to have the situation in Namibia under control. In this perspective, pragmatism becomes not a meeting of minds, as some Western governments and multinationals would have it, but a source of conflict between two political-economic adversaries.

"Except for Angola and Tanzania," says SADCC, "every economy in the region is dependent to a significant extent on RSA for sources of supply, key personnel, markets, finance, transportation, enterprises and/or employment. For Lesotho, Swaziland, and Namibia, the degree of subordinated economic integration is in some respects more like that of the outland provinces of a single state than of even an extreme dependence of weaker independent states." At a SADCC meeting in Maputo in 1980, President Samora Machel of Mozambique went further and said that southern Africa's dependence on South Africa was not an unplanned phenomenon:

> The economies of the Southern African countries were conceived and organised as functions of South Africa. South Africa was transformed into the zone's pole of attraction. All the road and rail networks converge there. Labour from the countries in the region was channelled there, paid derisory wages and submitted to an inhuman and racist regime. South Africa became the supply centre for raw materials, equipment and services for the subordinate industries that existed in the region. Through this process, that goes back to when the system of colonial exploitation was organised at the end of the last century, our countries were subordinated to South Africa and economically fettered to the dungeons of apartheid. This dependence is a fundamental influence in the under-development of our countries.[6]

Some economists reject this interpretation of economic history as attributing too much to Machiavellian calculations by imperialists and not enough to the free play of market forces; as belittling the contribution that capitalism has made to African development; and as being flavored too heavily with rhetoric. But they are arguing against a perception that is widely held in black Africa of how the region developed. There can be little disagreement with the words spoken by Machel at his country's independence: "The first day of our political independence is the first day of the longer and harder struggle for economic independence."[7]

Sir Seretse Khama, the late president of Botswana, believed that where there were no options for a government, the process of decision making was an empty one. He said:

> There is a need for choice of transportation routes and communications channels, for choice of sources of energy, for choice of markets and of suppliers, for choice of investment sources and enterprise partners. We need to develop programmes to reduce one-sided dependence and to increase the options open to our national economies and governments. This need is probably greater and more urgent in Southern Africa than anywhere else in the world. The fragmentation of our economies and their enforced integration into that of the Republic of South Africa have created an excessive national and regional dependence on that country which we seek to reduce.[8]

If southern Africa is sensitive to its dependence on South Africa, South Africa is equally conscious of its ability to capitalize on the situation. Even without the implementation of the constellation concept to institutionalize dependence, South Africa has been increasingly using its maize surplus and railway rolling stock—to mention only two economic pressure points—to drive home the reality of dependence. From Pretoria the cry is often heard these days that "Africa is dying," that it is sinking into poverty and falling standards of living, while South Africa stands solid. This view is epitomized in a report in *The South African Foundation News*, which quoted government leaders in Lesotho, Botswana, Mozambique, and Zambia as admitting that they could not afford to support sanctions against South Africa because their countries were too dependent on it: "It is difficult for us to cut the umbilical cord with South Africa," said Zambia's President Kenneth Kaunda in 1980. "It is plain trade . . . is going to grow."[9]

The article claims

> For the truth behind Africa's rhetorical smoke-screen is exploding trade with and dependence on South Africa. At least 49 of the countries do business with the white South; more than a dozen would be in serious trouble without South African food. . . . Eleven major wars and 53 coups since independence have left the continent in such a desperate state that it now has half the world's refugees. Perhaps nowhere has

Africa's retrogression and decay been more tragically highlighted than in its dwindling food production—a staggering 15 per cent since 1965. The people of Africa are set to double their numbers, to 800 million, within the next 19 years, yet there is no sign of levelling out of plummeting food production . . . South Africa is one of only half-a-dozen net food exporting nations in the world. In recent years it has been able to export 20 per cent of its food production, feeding not only its immediate neighbours but even its most ardent critics deep into the continent.

South Africa is responsible for 25 per cent of Africa's GNP, 40 per cent of industrial production, 45 per cent of the value of mining output, 66 per cent of the steel and 64 per cent of the electricity consumed. . . . The South African transport infrastructure, in terms of per capita contribution by transport sector to the GDP, is eight times larger than the rest of the countries in Africa south of the equator and South Africa has six of the 15 major harbours in the sub-continent. . . . More than a million black people in Southern African countries rely on jobs in South Africa for their income. Transfers and remittances by these guest workers, similar to the *gastarbeiter* in West Germany, probably exceeds R 1 billion a year. . . . For every worker who has a paid job in Lesotho there are six who have paid jobs in South Africa.[10]

These comments need balancing: a World Bank table shows overall agricultural production to have grown at 1.3 percent per year during the 1970s and food production to have fallen in only five of thirty-nine countries. But, one does not need to accept such a forbidding statistical background at face value to see that a SWAPO government would face a severe challenge if it tried to introduce socialism in Namibia. Probably its most pressing problem would be the need for skills. Due to the neglect of black education, only 3 percent of black children go past Form I; the territory produces fewer than 100 black matriculants a year; and no more than 300 black university graduates are thought to be scattered around the world. Population statistics are unreliable (the official 1980 estimate is 971,800, compared with the United Nations Institute for Namibia's estimate for the same year of 1,360,000).

If a figure of 105,000 is taken for the white population, it probably divides into two groups: 55,000 settlers and 50,000 expatriates. Namibia therefore could be denuded of half of its white population. Economically active whites number 42,000, of whom about 20,000 are civil servants. Already, skilled and semiskilled whites are leaving Namibia at a steady pace: farmers who have sold their land have moved to South Africa, school leavers and students, and local authority staff. The exodus is not on the scale of even the early white emigration from Zimbabwe, but this situation could exist because many Namibians are in a position to leave the decision whether to quit or stay to the last moment. Many civil servants have a fall-back position in South Africa; for all, and particularly important for farmers and businessmen, there are no restrictions on the expatriation of capital or assets to South Africa. A white flight, if it occurred, could be both sudden and disastrous, although a huge international pool exists from which expatriate officials, technicans, and others could be recruited.

One way in which SWAPO-in-exile is preparing for independence is by reproducing, in its various refugee centers, the educational, health, agricultural, and public-administration methods that it would implement in an independent Namibia. External programs run by SWAPO (including its own schools in Zambia and Angola) now include up to 4,000 students, from the artisan to university-degree levels.

SWAPO also participates in the United Nations's Nationhoood Program and has gained membership in most United Nations's agencies through its Council for Namibia. "The ability of SWAPO to obtain finance for this wide range of research and training projects, now costing about R 20 million, excluding direct support for refugees, is an index of the priority it places on non-military preparations for independence, as well as the strong international commitment to this aspect of SWAPO's activity." The United Nations Institute for Namibia in Lusaka trains about 300 middle-level administrators a year, seconding about 100 of them to African governments for further training.[11]

In Namibia itself, the Academy for Tertiary Education, which enrolls about 1,200 students a year, ranging from Form III to a cultural-enrichment course, is presently training more than 200 apprentices sent by nineteen firms, while companies, particularly the mining companies, have expanded their in-house training. Consolidated Diamond Mines, Ltd. (CDM) for example, has built a technical college for blacks in Ovamboland. Namibia, admittedly, has a small population, but the output of trained and experienced personnel nevertheless is pitifully small. Only about 600 white civil servants reportedly have opted to become part of the 4,500- to 5,000-strong Namibian civil service; the rest, mostly so-called guaranteed personnel, do not have to make up their minds for another two or three years, or even longer.

There is an urgent need for teachers, including teachers qualified to instruct in English (which, under SWAPO, would be the lingua franca, replacing Afrikaans). A Namibia Institute estimate of the expatriate professional and technical personnel that Namibia would need during the postindependence transition ranges as high as 17,500 (the Institute expects most whites to leave), which would cost R 180 million, and many are likely to be South Africans. Besides the farming, civil service, technical, and other skilled personnel Namibia would be seeking, it would also want "large numbers of commercial and central bankers, insurance staff and staff for other financial institutions."[12]

In Angola and Mozambique, Namibia has examples of the effect of an exodus of skills on agricultural production. In Mozambique's first year of independence, the flight of skilled workers led to a 70 percent decline in agricultural and industrial output. From being a net food exporter, the former Portuguese colony had to import 350,000 tons of food in 1979, almost all of it from South Africa. Agriculture's contribution to Namibia's GDP, following the drought, is down to 12.2 percent. Agriculture is divided into subsistence farming—in which 48 percent of the black labor force is engaged, and which contributes only 2.1 percent to GDP—and commercial farming, which is almost entirely in white hands. Agriculture's small contribution to GDP is due partly to the recent drought, but more especially to the rapid growth in mining's share, with the opening of the Rössing uranium mine, and greatly increased diamond earnings before the current slump.

Only 2 percent of Namibia's 83-million hectares (1 hectare = 2.5 acres) is suitable for crop cultivation (arable farming constitutes only 2 percent of agricultural production) and more than half of the territory is desert: Namibia's dependence on South Africa for food is therefore critical. Whites own 38-million hectares of the best agricultural and ranching land; and blacks own 33-million hectares of largely arid and sandy soils unsuitable for cultivation. White commercial farming consists of 5,100 farms: approximately 40 percent of these whites are German-speaking and the rest speak Afrikaans. An estimated 40 percent of white farmers use advanced technology; they would not easily be replaced.

A SWAPO government, pledged to land redistribution, would have to resolve a painful dilemma. In 1979, out of a GDP of R 1.4 billion only a little less than R 30 million was spread among 250,000 subsistence farmers and their dependents. This meager income was supplemented by earnings received from contract wage labor, but, in all, the income of blacks was only 12 percent of the GDP, compared with 24 percent for whites, the rest going to businesses or to South Africa.

SWAPO's Political Program envisages "a comprehensive agrarian transformation aimed at giving land to the tiller; the establishment of state-owned ranching and crop farms, aimed at making Namibia an agriculturally self-sufficient nation." But this goal would necessarily be a middle- and long-term program, as agricultural reform always is. Emigration of some unproductive white farmers would make some land available for redistribution, provided that the money can be found to buy it as in Zimbabwe, but not enough, and meanwhile the pressures on a SWAPO government to redress what it has called colonial land robbery would build up relentlessly.[13]

A SWAPO government's policy, based on the Zimbabwean example, would be to let productive white farmers continue without interference, although SWAPO would expect them to assist with the training of black farmers. In 1978, SWAPO's publicity secretary, Mokganedi Tlhabanello, said that there would have to be "some agreement between those who have land and those who don't"; this tentative approach to the problem has not changed much since that time. There is a striking contrast between the vocabulary of denunciation in *To Be Born a Nation* and the limited reforms for which SWAPO unavoidably would have to settle. The emphasis would be on less political aims: expanding the infrastructure, improving the water supply, increasing agricultural training, and, perhaps, reducing the influence of tribal elites.[14]

The small size of Namibia's population should enhance the possibilities for redistribution of land and wealth, but a SWAPO government nevertheless would have to proceed cautiously. Its priorities would have to be practical rather than ideological, with national unity and orderly development at the top of the list. Pragmatism, in fact, would be the only course of action. SWAPO knows that Namibia cannot detach itself completely from South Africa, in the foreseeable future, without ruinous consequences and that disengagement will be possible only when it can be done with economic and political safety. Much as it goes against the grain, SWAPO will have to regard its Political Program more as a broad guideline than as a detailed and binding course of action.

SWAPO's fiercest invective has been reserved for the transnationals operating in Namibia, which it sees as South Africa's "allies in exploitation." The Institute estimated in 1977 that 36 percent of Namibia's GDP (R 425 million) was being remitted abroad as profits, salaries, taxes, and state-enterprise surpluses, leaving a gross national income available for use inside the territory of less than two-thirds of its actual output.[15]

To Be Born a Nation singles out the attitudes of CDM as being more acceptable than many. Its following critical comment needs to be modified in the light of the present severe cutback in production (which was introduced for reasons connected with the weak international diamond market):

> As the prospect of independence draws nearer, the transnationals have been stepping up production from their mines so as to strip the country bare before a government of the people can bring its natural resources under its control. . . . This is the very core of imperialism, when corporate capital, hitting upon a lucrative resource (diamonds, uranium, oil), chooses not to spend or reinvest its vast profits locally but to export them to the industrial centres where its political power is assured.[16]

Rio Tinto Zinc (RTZ), among other equity participants, holds 46.5 percent of Rössing uranium mine, 13.2 percent is held by South Africa's parastatal Industrial Development Corporation (IDC), and 6.5 percent by the Afrikaner-controlled General Mining and Finance Corporation of South Africa. Mining in Namibia contributes 52 percent of GDP; in 1979-1980, approximately 80 percent of mining output, 45 percent of GDP, and 75 percent of export value; and 40 to 45 percent of the government's revenues came from two mining enterprises alone, Rössing and CDM. These two are the dominant multinational corporations with which SWAPO would have to negotiate.

Some seventeen companies, all foreign based, hold the major and usually complete ownership in the eighteen significant mines in Namibia. Ten are U.S.-based mining corporations, three are South African-based houses founded on British and South African capital, and two are South African parastatals, IDC and Iscor (Iron and Steel Corporation). The smaller mines usually are run by a single locally registered company, the major exception being the Tsumeb copper corporation, which owns one large and three medium-sized mines. Most of these companies are bound directly to their parent corporations as majority or wholly owned subsidiaries.

SWAPO's criticism of Namibia's economy is that "capitalist exploitation" has created a "grotesque imbalance," with farming, fishing, and mining (which are almost wholly in white hands) accounting for 97 percent of commercial primary production. Ruinous overfishing by South African-based companies and depletion of deep-sea resources by foreign vessels (particularly Soviet and Spanish), in what should be one of the three richest fishing grounds in the world, has had disastrous consequences. The neglect of the manufacturing sector (its contribution to GDP was less than 5 percent in 1980) has perpetuated the dependence on South African imports: 95 percent of everything consumed or invested in Namibia is imported, about two thirds of the imports originate in South Africa, and fully two fifths of the imports from other countries are routed through South Africa. Eighty percent of cattle exports are sent live by rail to South Africa, and karakul pelts are shipped in their raw state. Meat frozen or canned for export is handled by the processing facilities of two Afrikaner-owned companies in South Africa. Of the R 1.8 billion invested in the means of production in the three export sectors (mining, agriculture, and fishing) and related processing industries and suppliers, not more than R 40 million is owned by local interests, and hardly any by black Namibians.

South Africa's economic grip on Namibia is a stranglehold: it owns the rail-transport system, the airline, the entire communications network, and the only viable port (Walvis Bay); it supplies the territory's oil, and coal; most civil servants are South Africans and could be withdrawn; Namibia is knitted into the Rand Monetary Area and the Southern African Customs Union; and, until independence, there will probably be no exchange control. To compound this dependency, the world recession has caused markets for Namibia's uranium, diamonds, and base metals to shrink; a devastating drought, the worst since 1933, has caused huge stock losses; unemployment is growing; and, for as long as the "illegal" South African regime occupies Namibia, investment and aid will not be forthcoming from multinational corporations and foreign governments.

In spite of the formidable economic constraints that will operate after independence, a SWAPO government would owe it to its followers to make certain minimum changes, which, however, will add to the apprehensions of the whites and probably cause more of them to leave: for example, elimination of residual apartheid (in schools, hospitals, swimming pools, and so forth); rejection of Afrikaans as the "language of the oppressor" (the Institute's term), and the establishment of English as the lingua franca; acceptance of embassies, trade, and advisers from Eastern-bloc countries; and membership in the OAU and SADCC, and other demonstrations of solidarity with black Africa. Independence would bring its own ethos in which whites would realize that they were no longer the masters, and the question of how many whites would adjust to this situation is one of the imponderables in the Namibian equation.

SWAPO has given a fairly explicit indication of the policies that it would pursue after independence. Neither nationalization of major enterprises nor confiscation of smaller businesses is contemplated. There will be no dismissals or expulsions of competent white farmers, civil servants, or technical personnel—if they accept the laws of the country. Probably taking Zimbabwe as its model, SWAPO would make every effort to limit the flight of skilled personnel.

The Program foresees a postindependence transition period with mixed state, cooperative, private, and joint ownership of the country's productive forces. Partial public ownership of key sectors of the economy—mining, fishing, banking and finance, ranching, and agriculture—seems likely. Titles to nonproductive assets, such as homes and savings accounts, and other basic property rights of this kind, appear to be assured. The title to productive assets such as fish, minerals, and land will be regarded as the property of the nation, although private occupancy, use, and deveopment of such assets will not necessarily be excluded. South African state corporations will probably be subject to nationalization without compensation.

> Overall economic strategy has as a goal comprehensive agrarian reform in the interests of food security and rural development. Meat and fish industries, for example, would be partially diverted from export to internal consumption, and new processing industries sponsored. . . . Mining is seen as a key source of foreign exchange and surplus for the public sector to finance services and investment in rural development.

SWAPO and the Postindependence Era

SWAPO intends to keep all major mines running using a combination of management contracts and joint ventures to preserve technical efficiency and the generation of surplus over an indefinite, but moderately extended period. . . . The diamond industry in Botswana and Tanzania provides an implicit model. SWAPO has quite specifically stated that post-independence involvement by transnationals is acceptable, subject to its being on agreed terms which sageguard Namibian foreign exchange, profitability, employment, traning and overall economic control.[17]

Any assessment of Namibia's future could include a number of doomsday scenarios, but one assumption that has been made is that if South Africa were to agree to independence, and SWAPO controlled the government, then coexistence—even if only in an uneasy way—would be possible. The reasoning behind this assumption is that it would not be in South Africa's interest to destabilize a regime that it had permitted to be established: in the eyes of South Africa's supporters, such a course would compound the felony. It might therefore be possible to establish a tenuous working relationship between Namibia and South Africa that could provide a base upon which SWAPO could build.

A move would be made to call a donors' conference of the kind that was held in Zimbabwe. Although the present recessionary climate is not conducive to liberal aid programs, and the cost of the United Nations's peacekeeping force (UNTAG) that will be based in Namibia over the transition period will be huge, it has been noted that, in the first eighteen months of Zimbabwe's independence, the United States alone gave $55 million. West Germany, too, might feel an obligation to donate generously to its former colony, and aid would be given by various other countries, particularly Sweden. The contribution that the churches will be able to make should not be overlooked, either.

Namibia could also join the Lomé Convention, thereby gaining access to European Economic Community (EEC) markets and to aid programs for the development of social and industrial infrastructures. Although financing the national debt has become prohibitive (as Poland has discovered), aid prospects for Namibia are by no means discouraging. Its economy can be described as promising, if precarious. It is not just a wretchedly poor African country; it is mineral rich, with a small population.

SADCC takes an optimistic view of the future in another area:

Namibia has numerous real possibilities for restructuring its economy away from RSA dependence. As Namibia establishes its own central bank and its own currency it could leave the RMA [Rand Monetary Area] with little difficulty, invest its foreign assets in currencies of its own choice, introduce its own exchange control regulations and conduct an independent monetary policy. There is no question that this can or should be done; the only issue is how soon? An important problem is likely to be that of capital flight when liberation looks imminent, but there is little that can be done about that.[18]

During the Geneva conference on Namibia in 1981, SWAPO indicated that the sale of uranium oxide from the Rössing mine to European nuclear-power plants would be continued according to economic, not political, criteria. This statement has been interpreted as implying the retention of an external management, although not necessarily that of RTZ, the principal owners.

SWAPO's view is that RTZ's establishment of the Rössing mine was illegal after 1966, when the United Nations General Assembly formally revoked South Africa's mandate over Namibia and assumed sovereignty for the territory. Further, in 1974, the United Nations Council for Namibia issued a decree prohibiting further exploitation of the territory's resources and stipulating that a future Namibian government could claim damages from any company that did so. Would a SWAPO government risk tampering with the management of Rössing in the postindependence period? It might have more pressing matters to attend to. Nearly all of the key jobs at Rössing are held by 900 white employees; there would be good reason not to upset them.

Fitting Rössing and CDM into a new order in Namibia would be a delicate operation. Negotiating with any multinational company, with its serried ranks of experts, is an intimidating experience. A SWAPO government would be able to seek help from the United Nations and from the British Commonwealth's Technical Assistance Group, each of which has personnel available for such negotiations, but, even with this professional support, a SWAPO government would not lightly seek a confrontation. Later, however, it might wish to emulate Zimbabwe's example and set up a state-owned minerals-marketing corporation.

There is a further crucial area in which South Africa would not hesitate to use its economic levers to further its interests—security. SWAPO has given an assurance that it would not permit the exiled African National Congress of South Africa (ANC) to establish guerrilla bases in Namibia, but Pretoria regards the distinction between *bases* and an ANC presence in the form of an *office* as academic: it sees each as a source of subversion. Yet for SWAPO to deny a place to the ANC would be an impairment of its manhood in Africa. The situation would not be an easy one to resolve.

There would also be the question of a Soviet presence in Namibia. When SWAPO started its liberation struggle, the only countries prepared to help militarily were Eastern-bloc nations, and, theoretically, after independence the Soviets should have influence with a SWAPO government. But there are other factors to consider. Walvis Bay, the only port where the Soviets might establish a naval presence, is in South African hands, SWAPO, like any other African government, would be more concerned with establishing genuine independence than with parceling itself out to either South Africa or to the Soviet Union. A prominent Soviet role in Namibia would sharpen the conflict with the United States and, in the present deteriorating international climate, such a policy would incur too great a risk. African regimes, in Moscow's experience, are notoriously unstable, making it not worthwhile to invest heavily in them. Even after independence, as Andrew Young, former U.S. Ambassador to the United Nations, once expressed it, the Soviet Union could not compete with the West in providing the goodies. Vassily Solodovnikov, former director of the Africa Institute in Moscow, and former Soviet Ambassador to Zambia, confirmed this conclusion in 1976 when he said: "A specific feature of the development of the socialist-orientated countries in Africa is that even after their choice of the noncapitalist way they are still in the orbit of the world capitalist economic system."[19]

The extent of Soviet involvement in Namibia would be determined as much by Pretoria as by Windhoek: South Africa could use its economic leverage in Namibia to limit the Soviet presence. Soviet influence, therefore, is not likely to reach its height in southern Africa until South Africa itself passes into ANC or other black hands. Then, many of the constraints that emanate from South Africa today, and extend through southern Africa, might fall away, and the Soviet Union may be able to move more freely in the region. If this reading of the situation is correct, a SWAPO victory in Namibia will not make a significant difference to the contemporary Soviet role in southern Africa. Indeed, it has been argued that a SWAPO victory will reduce the contemporary Soviet role, because, once Namibia is independent, the last colonial occupation will have ended, and South Africa's neighbors will look for a period of peace in which to rebuild their economies.

Notes

1. Amon J. Nsekela (ed.), *Southern Africa: Toward Economic Liberation* (London, 1981), 62. Reprinted with permission of Rex Collings.
2. Ibid., 3.
3. SWAPO Publicity Committee, *To Be Born a Nation: The Liberation Struggle for Namibia* (London, 1981).
4. Ibid., 258.
5. *Observer*, (February 3, 1982), 9.
6. Nskela, *Southern Africa*, 12; Aloysius Kgarebe (ed.), *SADCC*

2—*Maputo* (Nottingham, 1981), 24. Reprinted with permission of Aloysius Kgarebe, chairman of SADCC Liaison Commission.

7. Nsekela, *Southern Africa,* vii.
8. Nsekela, *Southern Africa,* ix.
9. Special Report by David Braun, *South Africa Foundation News* (March 1981), 2. Reprinted with permission.
10. Ibid.
11. Catholic Institute for International Relations and British Council of Churches, Namibia in the 1980s (London, 1981), 53. Reprinted with permission.
12. Nsekela, *Southern Africa,* 108.
13. SWAPO *To Be Born a Nation,* 45.
14. *Financial Mail* (August 11, 1978).
15. SWAPO, *To Be Born a Nation,* 43.
16. Ibid., 49.
17. Catholic Institute, *Namibia in the 1980s,* 54–55.
18. Nsekela, *Southern Africa,* 107.
19. David E. Albright (ed.), *Communism in Africa* (Bloomington, 1980), 43.

Bibliography

Adam, Heribert, *Modernizing Racial Domination* (Berkeley, 1971).
Amelunxen, Clemens, "New Development in South West Africa," *Plural Societies,* V (1974), 3–8.
Ballinger, Robert B., *South West Africa: The Case against the Union* (Johannesburg, 1961).
Banghart, P.D., "The Effects of the Migrant Labourer on the Ovambo of South West Africa," *Fort Hare Papers,* V (1972), 265–281.
Beiderweiden, H., "Wollschaftszucht in Deutsch-Sudwestafrika," *Vierteljahrschr. Sozial-u. Wirtschaftsgesch,* I (1971).
Berg, Elliot, et al., *Namibia: Economic Growth, Structure, and Prospects* (Ann Arbor, 1976).
Berthold, W.S., *Namibia's Economic Potential and Existing Economic Ties with the Republic of South Africa* (Berlin, 1977).
Bissell, Richard, and Chester Crocker (eds.), *South Africa into the 1980s* (Boulder, 1980).
Brandt, H. et al., *Perspectives of Independent Development in Southern Africa: The Cases of Zimbabwe and Namibia* (Berlin, 1980).
Bridgman, Jon M., *The Revolt of the Hereroes* (London, 1981).
Bruwer, J.P. van S., *Southwest Africa: The Disputed Land* (Cape Town, 1966).
Butcher, Goler Teal, "Reflections on U.S. Policy towards Namibia," *Issue,* IV (1974), 59–62.
Catholic Institute for International Relations, *Namibia in the 1980s* (London, 1981).
Christie, Renfrew, "Who Benefits by the Kunene Hydro-Electric Schemes?" *Social Dynamics,* II (1976), 31–43.
Cockram, G.-M., *South West African Mandate* (Cape Town, 1976).
Collett, Sue, "The Human Factor in the Economic Development of Namibia," *Optima,* XXVIII (1980), 191–219.
Commonwealth Secretariat, *The Mineral Industry of Namibia: Perspectives for Independence* (London, 1978).
Crocker, Chester A., "South Africa: Strategy for Change," *Foreign Affairs,* LIX (1980), 323–351.
Crocker, Chester A., and Penelope Hartland-Thunberg, *Namibia at the Crossroads: Economic and Political Prospects* (Washington, D.C., 1978).
Cronje, Gillian, and Suzanne Cronje, *The Workers of Namibia* (London, 1979).
Crowell, W.M., *The Evolution of South African Control over South Africa* (Ann Arbor, 1977).

Dale, Richard, "The Ambiguities of Self-Determination for South West Africa, 1918–1939: A Concept or a Symbol of Decolonization," *Plural Societies,* IV (1973), 29–57.

———, "The 'Glass Palace War' over the International Decolonization of South-West Africa," *International Organization,* XXIX (1975), 535–544.

———, "The Armed Forces as an Instrument of South African Policy in Namibia," *Journal of Modern African Studies,* XVIII (1980), 57–71.

———, "South Africa and Namibia: Changing the Guard and Guarded Change," *Current History,* LXXVI (1979), 101–104, 136–137.

———, "Political Changes in Namibia, Botswana, and Swaziland," *Current History,* LXXI (1976), 161–164, 183.

———, "South Africa and Namibia," *Current History,* LXXIII (1977), 209–213, 226–227.

Davis, John, and James Baker (eds.), *Southern Africa in Transition* (New York, 1966).

De Lange, E.J. Roukens, *South-West Africa, 1946–1960: A Selective Bibliography* (Cape Town, 1961).

De Vries, J. Lukas, *Mission and Colonialism in Namibia* (Johannesburg, 1978).

Drechsler, Horst, *"Let Us Die Fighting"—The Struggle of the Herero and Nama against German Imperialism, 1884–1915* (London, 1980).

Dugard, John, "The Revocation of the Mandate for South-West Africa," *American Journal of International Law,* LXII (1968), 78–97.

———, "South West Africa and the 'Terrorist Trial,' " *American Journal of International Law,* LXIV (1970), 19–41.

———, *The South West Africa/Namibia Dispute* (Berkeley, 1973).

Du Pisani, André, "Namibia: The Search for Alternatives," *South Africa International,* XII (1981), 292–303.

———, *Namibia since Geneva* (Johannesburg, 1981).

———, "Reflections on the Role of Ethnicity in the Politics of Namibia," *Plural Societies,* VIII (1977), 79–98.

Esterhuyse, J.H., *South West Africa, 1880–1894* (Cape Town, 1968).

Falk, Richard, "South West Africa Cases: An Appraisal," *International Organization,* XXI (1967), 1–23.

Ferreira, Eduardo, "International Capital in Namibia," *Ufahamu* (Fall, 1972).

First, Ruth, *Southwest Africa* (Baltimore, 1963).

Fonni, Dean, "South Africa: The Evolving Experience," in James Roberts (ed.), *Defense Policy Formation* (Durham, 1980).

Gebhardt, F.B., "The Socio-economic Status of Farm Labourers in Namibia," *South African Labour Bulletin*, IV (1978), 145–173.

Gibson, Richard, *African Liberation Movements* (New York, 1972).

Goldblatt, I., *The Mandated Territory of South-West Africa in Relation to the United Nations* (Cape Town, 1961).

———, *The Conflict between the United Nations and the Union of South Africa in Regard to South West Africa* (Cape Town, 1961).

Gordon, Robert J., *Mines, Masters, and Migrants: Life in a Namibian Compound* (Johannesburg, 1977).

Gottschalk, K., "South African Labour Policy in Namibia, 1915–1975," *South African Labour Bulletin*, IV (1978), 75–106.

Green, L.C., "South West Africa and the World Court," *International Journal*, XXII (1966), 39–67.

Green, Reginald H., "Transition to What? Some Issues of Freedom and Necessity in Namibia," *Development and Change*, XI (1980), 419–454.

———, "The Unforgiving Land—Basis for a Post-Independence Liberation Programme in Namibia," *IDS Bulletin*, XI (1980), 70–76.

———, *"Namibia: A Political Economy Survey* (Sussex, 1979).

———, *Manpower Estimates and Development Implications for Namibia* (Lusaka, 1978).

———, M.L. Kiljunen, and K.K. Kuljunen (eds.), *Namibia: The Last Colony* (London, 1981).

Gross, Ernest A., "The South-West Africa Case: What Happened?" *Foreign Affairs*, XXXXV (1966), 36–48.

Groth, S., "The Condemnation of Apartheid by the Churches in South-West Africa," *International Review of Missions*, LXI (1972), 183–195.

Grundy, Kenneth, *Confrontation and Accommodation in Southern Africa* (Berkeley, 1973).

———, *Guerrilla Struggle in Southern Africa* (New York, 1971).

Harvey, C.E., *The Rio Tinto Company: An Economic History of a Leading International Mining Concern, 1873–1954* (London, 1981).

Hendriks, Colleen, "Sam Nujoma: Profile of SWAPO's Leader," *Munger Africana Library*, XI (1980).

Henriksen, Thomas H., "Namibia: A Comparison with Anti-Portuguese Insurgency," *Round Table*, LXX (1980), 184–194.

Hevener, N.K., "The 1971 South-West African Opinion—A New International Juridical Philosophy," *International and Comparative Law Quarterly*, XXIV (1975), 791–810.

Hidayatullah, M., *The South West Africa Case* (London, 1967).

Higgens, Rosalyn, "The International Court and South-West Africa: The Implications of the Judgment," *International Affairs,* XLII (1966), 573–599.

Highet, K., "The South-West Africa Cases," *Current History,* LII (1967), 154–161.

Horrell, Muriel, *South-West Africa* (Johannesburg, 1967).

Hunke, Heinz, *Namibia: The Strength of the Powerless* (Rome, 1980).

Imishue, R.W., *South-West Africa: An International Problem* (London, 1965).

Innes, Duncan, "Imperialism and the National Struggle in Namibia," *Review of African Political Economy,* III (1979), 44–59.

Johnson, R.W., *How Long Will South Africa Survive?* (New York, 1978).

Kahn, E.J., Jr., "A Reporter at Large: Who Cares? . . . We Do!" *The New Yorker* (June 25, 1979), 60–88.

Kane-Berman, John, *Contract Labour in South-West Africa* (Johannesburg, 1972).

Kiljunen, K., "Namibia: The Ideology of National Liberation," *IDS Bulletin,* XI (1980), 65–71.

Kleist, Karsten E.B. von, *Förderung des Tourismus als Beitrag zur gesamtwirtschaftlichen und gesamtgesellschaftlichen Entwicklung von SWA/Namibia* (Oxford, 1980).

Konrat, Georg von, *Passport to Truth: Inside South West Africa: An Astounding Story of Oppression* (London, 1972).

Kooy, Marcelle, "The Contract Labor System and the Ovambo Crisis of 1971 in South-West Africa," *African Studies Review,* XVI (1973), 83–105.

Kozonguizi, F. Jariretundu, "South-West Africa: Historical Background and Current Problems," in John A. Davis and James K. Baker (eds.), *Southern Africa in Transition* (New York, 1966), 45–58.

Krogh, D.C., "The National Income and Expenditure of South-West Africa," *South African Journal of Economics,* XXVIII (1960), 3–22.

Kröner, A.W., *Namibië—Een Testcase voor Zuid-Afrika* ('s-Gravenhage, 1981).

Lacoste, François, "Le Sud-ouest africain—Namibie en 1979," *Politique Internationale,* III (1979), 251–281.

Landis, Elizabeth, "Namibia: Impending Independence?" in Gwendolen M. Carter and Patrick O'Meara (eds.), *Southern Africa in Crisis* (Bloomington, 1977), 163–199.

Lawrie, Gordon, "New Light on South-West Africa: Some Extracts from and Comments on the Odendaal Report," *African Studies,* XXIII (1964), 105–119.

Lazar, Leonard, *Namibia* (London, 1972).

Lefort, P., "Namibie en lutte," *Communisme,* III (1973), 61–74.

Bibliography

Leistner, E., et al., *Namibia/SWA Prospectus* (Pretoria, 1980).
Lemarchand, René (ed.), *American Policy in South Africa: The Stakes and the Stance* (Washington, D.C., 1978).
Levinson, Olga, *The Story of Namibia* (Cape Town, 1976).
Lissner, Jorgen (ed.), *Namibia 1975: Hope, Fear and Ambiguity* (Geneva, 1976).
Louis, William Roger, "The South West African Origins of the 'Sacred Trust,' 1914–1919," *African Affairs*, LXVI (1967), 20–39.
Louw, Walter, *Owambo* (Sandton, 1977).
Malan, J.S., *Peoples of South West Africa/Namibia* (Pretoria, 1980).
Manning, C.A.W., "South West Africa and the World Court: A Comment on World Consultation," *Plural Societies*, II (1971), 17–29.
Melber, Henning, *Schule und Kolonialismus: Das Formale Erziehungswesen Namibias* (Hamburg, 1979).
———, "The South West Africa Cases: A Personal Analysis," *International Relations*, III (1966), 98–110.
Moorsom, Richard J.B., *The Origins of the Contract Labour System in Namibia, 1900–1926* (York, 1980).
———, "Labour Consciousness and the 1971–1972 Contract Workers' Strike in Namibia," *Development and Change*, X (1979), 205–231.
———, "Migrant Workers and the Formation of SWANLA, 1900–1920," *South African Labour Bulletin*, IV (1978).
———, "Underdevelopment, Contract Labour and Worker Consciousness in Namibia, 1915–1972," *Journal of Southern African Studies*, IV (1977), 52–87.
Morris, M., *Armed Conflict in Southern Africa* (Cape Town, 1974).
Murray, Roger, *The Mineral Industry of Namibia: Perspectives for Independence* (London, 1979).
———, "Namibia's Elusive Independence: A Contest between African Nationalism and South African Interests," *Round Table*, LXVII (1977), 42–49.
———, "No Easy Path to Independence," *Africa Report*, XXII (1977), 17–21.
———, et al., *The Role of Foreign Firms in Namibia* (Uppsala, 1974).
Nielsen, Waldemar, *The Great Powers and Africa* (New York, 1969).
Obozuwa, A.U., *The Namibian Question: Legal and Political Aspects* (Benin City, 1973).
O'Callaghan, M., *Namibia: The Effects of Apartheid on Culture and Education* (Paris, 1977).
Odendaal, François, "Is There a Peaceful Solution to the SWA Conflict?" *Africa Institute Bulletin*, XVI (1978), 76–80.
Olivier, M.J., "Ethnic Relations in South-West Africa," *Plural Societies*, II (1971), 31–42.

Persaud, Motee, "Namibia and the International Court of Justice," *Current History*, LXVIII (1975), 220–225.
Pollock, A.J., "The South-West Africa Cases and the Jurisprudence of International Law," *International Organization*, XXIII (1969), 767–787.
Pomerance, Michla, "The Admission of Judges in Advisory Proceedings: Some Reflections in the Light of the Namibia Case," *American Journal of International Law*, LXVII (1973), 446–464.
Pool, Gerhardus, *Die Herero-Opstand, 1904–1907* (Cape Town, 1979).
Potholm, Christian P., "The Protectorates, the O.A.U. and South Africa," *International Journal*, XXII (1966), 68–72.
Potholm, Christian P., and Richard Dale (eds.), *Southern Africa in Perspective: Essays in Regional Politics* (New York, 1972).
Prinsloo, D.S., *Walvis Bay and the Penguin Islands: Background and Status (Pretoria, 1977)*.
Ramcharan, Bertie, "The South-West Africa Advisory Opinion of the World Court," *Millennium*, I (1972), 23–48.
Redekop, C.G., "The Limits of Diplomacy: The Case of Namibia," *International Journal*, XXXV (1979/1980), 70–90.
Roberts, James (ed.), *Defense Policy Formation* (Durham, 1980).
Roberts, M., "South-West Africa and the U.N.," *World Today*, XXII (1966), 407–410.
Rogerson, C.M., "A Future 'University of Namibia'? The Role of the U.N. Institute for Namibia," *Journal of Modern African Studies*, XVIII (1980), 675–683.
Rotberg, Robert I., *Suffer the Future: Policy Choices in Southern Africa* (Cambridge, Mass., 1980).
———, "Achieving the New Namibia: Incentives and Obstacles" (Cambridge, Mass., 1977).
———, "The New Namibia," *The Washington Quarterly*, I (1978), 13–25.
———, "Why Namibia Matters," *African Index*, V (1982), 1–4.
Rubin, Neville, *Labour and Discrimination in Namibia* (Geneva, 1977).
Seiler, John, "Namibian Negotiations: Hiatus or Collapse?" *The Seiler Report*, III (1980).
———(ed.), *Southern Africa since the Portuguese Coup* (Boulder, 1979).
Serfontein, J.H.P., *Namibia?* (Randburg, 1976).
Shaw, Timothy M., "Southern Africa: From Detente to Deluge?" in *Yearbook of World Affairs* (London, 1978), 117–138.
Slonim, Solomon, *South West Africa and the United Nations: An International Mandate in Dispute* (Baltimore, 1972).
Smith, D.E., "The International Community and the South West Africa Dispute," *Queen's Quarterly*, LXXIV (1967), 593–609.

Soehnge, G., *Tsumeb: A Historical Sketch* (Windhoek, 1967).
Spicer, Michael, "Namibia: Elusive Independence," *World Today*, XXXVI (1980), 406–414.
Steward, Alexander, *South-West Africa: The Sacred Trust* (Johannesburg, 1963).
SWAPO Publicity Committee, *To Be Born a Nation: The Liberation Struggle for Namibia* (London, 1981).
Thomas, Wolfgang H., "Independence and Beyond: Namibia's Future in Perspective" (Stellenbosch, 1981).
———, *Namibia: Beschäftingungstruktur und Arbeitskräftebedarf* (Berlin, 1979).
———, *Mittelfristige Entwicklungsperspektiven fur Namibia, Stiftung Wissenschaft und Politik* (Ebenhausen, 1978).
———, *Economic Development in Namibia: Towards Acceptable Development Strategies for Independent Namibia* (Munich, 1978).
Thompson, Leonard, and Jeffrey Butler (eds.), *Change in Contemporary South Africa* (Berkeley, 1975).
Tötemeyer, Gerhard H.K., *Namibia Old and New* (London, 1978).
———, *Ovamboland Emergent* (London, 1977).
———, Political Groupings in Namibia: Their Role and Chances," *International Affairs Bulletin*, II (1978), 23–31.
———, "The Potential Role of Political Parties in the Political Development of South West Africa," *The South African Journal of African Affairs*, VI (1976), 151–161.
———, *South West Africa/Namibia: Facts, Attitudes, Assessment, and Prospects* (Randburg, 1977).
Truebody, Charles T., *Labour Relations in South West Africa—A First Assessment* (Windhoek, 1982).
Umozurike, U.O., "The Namibia (South West Africa) Cases, 1950–1971," *African Quarterly*, XII (1972), 41–58.
Uys, Stanley, "The Prospects for an Independent Namibia," *Ditchley Conference Report*, X (1981).
Wiechers, Marinus, "South West Africa: The Background, Content, and Significance of the Opinon of the World Court of 21 June 1971," *Comparative International Law Journal of South Africa*, V (1972), 123–170.
Wellington, John H., *Southwest Africa and its Human Issues* (New York, 1967).
———, "South West Africa: The Facts about the Disputed Territory," *Optima*, XV (1965), 40–54.
Whitby, Jonathan, *Bundu Doctor* (New York, 1961).
Winter, Colin O'B., *Namibia* (Grand Rapids, 1977).

———, "Church and State in South West Africa," *South African Outlook,* CII (1972), 38–40.

Yarborough, William, *Trial in Africa* (Washington, D.C., 1976).

Index

Abattoirs, 65, 95–96
Abolition of Racial Discrimination (Urban Residential and Public Amenities) Act, 24
Abrahams, Kenneth, physician and politician, 36
Academy of Tertiary Education, Windhoek, 75, 106
Administrator-general, 20, 21, 22, 35, 74
Advisory Council (South-West Africa), 5
Advisory Council for Namibia, representation on, 14
Affirmative action, 72, 84
Africa: anticolonial voting in, 37; battle against apartheid, 19; countries in compared with Namibia, 67, 68 (table); development problems in rural areas, 60; economic dependency on South Africa, 101, 103, 104–105; independence in, 1, 7, 14, 15; and Namibian independence, 7, 29; refugee movements, 83–84; solidarity with, 110; Soviet influence, 113
Africa Institute, Moscow, 113
African Institute, Pretoria, 41
African National Congress of South Africa (ANC), 112, 113
Africans. *See* Blacks
Afrikaans language: English substituted for, 106, 110; whites speaking, 43, 74, 94, 107
Afrikaners, people, 2, 17, 38
Age, of population, 49 (table)
Aggenys, South Africa, 45
Agriculture: African production, 105; development strategies, 80, 84–85, 89, 95–96, 108; economic role, 55–60, 99, 107; exodus, 73, 85, 95; exports, 43, 55, 57, 69; physiography and, 30, 43, 45; stability of manpower, 94. *See also* Commercial farming; land; subsistence farming
Ahtisaari, Martti, of the U.N., 22
Airline, 44, 109
Airports, 43–44
Amnesty International, 16

Anchovies, 60
Anglo-Boer War, 2
Angola, 9, 29; Cuban troops in, 15, 32; exodus, 74, 107; independence, 14, 15; invasions by South Africa, 15, 25, 32; oil deposits, 30; refugees from, 83; relations with, 66, 96, 102; in SADCC, 101; and South Africa, 103; and Southern African Transport and Communication Commission, 97; and SWAPO, 20, 23, 24; SWAPO school in, 106
Apartheid, 8–9, 11, 19, 20, 110. *See also* Segregation
Arandis, town, 45, 64
Arsenic, 31, 62

Balance of payments, 67, 69 (table), 98
Base metals, 31, 54, 69, 110
Basters: advisory council, 8; percent in population, 30; representation in Advisory Council for Namibia, 14; revolt (1925), 4; and SWAPO, 8, 38; and Turnhalle Conference, 16, 18
Beef, 31
Beer breweries, 65
Belgium, 1
Blacks: and DTA, 38; education and training, 5, 75–77, 105, 106; effect of past socioeconomic developments, 87–88; exiles, 26, 77; health and welfare, 78–79; homelands, 8–9; housing, 77; income averages, 54; in industry and commerce, 96; investment in production, 109; land ownership, 4, 7, 57, 58; in population, 30, 49; and resolution of Namibian problem, 40; segregation, 3–4, 72–73, 79; in South-West African Territory Force, 26; subsistence farming, 55, 58–60, 107; suspicion of white settlers, 1–2; and SWAPO, 26, 37–38; taxation, 70; and transition to independence, 73–75, 80, 84–87, 88–89; and Turnhalle Conference,

123

16–17, 18; and white commercial farming, 4, 55, 57, 94, 95
Bondelswarts rebellion (1922), 4
Botha, Prime Minister Pieter W., 24, 33, 38, 39
Botha, Foreign Minister Roelof F., 25
Botswana, 38, 96, 111; in customs union, 98; Namibian railway link, 102; refugees from, 83; in SADCC, 101; and South Africa, 34, 103, 104; in Southern African Transport and Communication Commission, 97
Brazil, 6
British (people), 2
British Commonwealth, 98; Technical Assistance Group, 112. *See also* Great Britain
Broadcasting, 44
Budget, Namibian, 69–71, 79, 93, 97; table, 70
Bus lines, 43
Bushmen (San), 14, 16, 18, 30, 43

Cadmium, 31, 62
Caetano, Prime Minister Marcello, 14
Canada, 19, 36
Cape Colony, administration of Walvis Bay, 17
Cape Town, South Africa, 17, 95
Capital: need for, 65; outflow, 58, 69, 74, 106; in physical infrastructure, 67; and possible development strategies, 80, 81, 82
Caprivi: area, 16, 46; East, 8, 14, 16, 18; people, 30, 38; Strip, 24, 59
Carrington, Lord, British Foreign Secretary, 24
Carter, President Jimmy, administration, 19, 26, 29, 33, 35
Cassinga, Angola, massacre, 21, 23
Catering, 67
Cattle, 17, 30; grazing areas, 54, 58; production, 43, 55, 57, 95–96, 109
Census, official, 46
Chand, General Prem, 24
China, People's Republic of, 18
Christian, Jacobus, 4–5
Chromium, 30
Churches, aid from, 81, 111

Civil service, and transition to independence, 73–74, 105–106, 109
Clothing factories, 65
Coal, 44, 45, 62, 109
Coastline, strategic importance, 31
Collett, Sue, author, 41
Colonialism, 1–2, 4; voting against, 37
Coloured Affairs, Ministry of, 8
Coloureds, people, 8, 14, 18, 30, 43, 81
Commerce, 43, 67, 80; priorities in, 94, 96
Commercial farming, 55, 57–58, 59, 60, 107; and transition to independence, 73, 85, 94, 95
Communications, 43–44, 58, 67; South African dominance in, 96, 109
Communism, 29
Community and cultural amenities, segregation in, 72, 73
Community services, 67
Conference of East and Central African States (Lusaka), 21
Consolidated Diamond Mines, Ltd. (CDM), 30, 31, 64–65; education sponsored by, 75, 106; and SWAPO, 108, 109, 112
Constellation of States, 98, 99, 102
Construction, 66–67. *See also* Physical infrastructure
Consumer spending, 71, 80
Contact Group of Western Nations, 1, 19; proposals and negotiations, 20–22, 23–24, 36–37, 89, 94
Copper, 31, 43, 62, 64
Council for Namibia (SWAPO), 106
Cuba, troops in Angola, 15, 32
Curfew, 3
Customs union, 86, 98, 109
Cyprus, 22

Dairy products, 55
Damara, people, 8, 14, 16, 18, 30, 59; Council, 36; and DTA, 38; and SWAPO, 37, 38
Damaraland, 8, 36
De Beers Ltd., 30. *See also* Consolidated Diamond Mines.
Defense, 44; forces, 49, 51, 52; importance to South Africa, 32–33; spending, 71, 80

Index

Demilitarized zone, 24
Democratic Cooperative Party of Ovamboland (DEMCOP), 9
Democratic Turnhalle Alliance (DTA): as alternative to SWAPO, 34–36; elections and, 23, 26, 37, 38; formed, 20; government budget prospects, 71; government, and discrimination, 73; legislative power, 24; and transition to independence, 82
Desalination projects, 45
Development: agricultural and rural problems, 58–60; alternative strategies for, 79–87; assets and constraints (table), 47–48); GDP and, 52–54; of production, 95–96; social needs in, 71–79; of transport infrastructure, 97
Diamonds, 30, 43, 62, 107, 111; and balance of payments, 67; market shrinkage, 97, 110; prices, 54; tax revenues, 69. See also DeBeers
Discrimination. See Segregation
Ditchley conference, 93, 97, 99
Drought, 46, 54, 57, 58, 80, 95, 107, 110
DTA. See Democratic Turnhalle Alliance

Eastern Europe, possible ties with, 81, 110, 112
Economic Advisory Committee, 65
Economic cooperation, priority area, 98–99
Economy: and dependency of South Africa, 101–105, 109–110; development strategies, 79–87; independence and priorities in, 93–99; overview of, 41, 43; performance assessed, 67–71; problems for future government, 105–113; and resolution of impasse, 87–89. See also specific sectors
Education, 93; budget under mandate, 3, 5; efforts to expand, 66, 74, 75, 77, 88, 89, 94–95, 106; needs, 59, 78 (table); statistics on black, 105; and transition to independence, 81, 86; trends, 76 (table)
Elections: boycotts of, 9, 23; of 1978, 23, 35; internationally supervised, question of, 88–89; proposed by Contact Group, 20, 22, 25; prospects, and SWAPO, 36–37, 39
Electricity, 44–45, 58
Elf Aquitaine mine, 64
Elifas, Chief Filemon, 9
Embargo, proposed (1975), 15–16
Emigration. See Exodus
Employment and unemployment: in agriculture, 50, 51, 55, 57–58, 99; by category, 51 (table); changes in opportunities, 51 (table); construction, 66; development strategies and, 80, 85; fishing, 62; industry and commerce, 96; labor supply and, 50–52, 71, 96; mining, 64; and reduction in discrimination, 72; by sector, 50 (table); services, 67; unemployment increase, 110
Energy resources, 44–45, 65
Engineering works, 65
English: as established language, 110; teachers in, 106; whites speaking, 43, 74
Ethiopia, 7, 9
Etosha Pan, 30, 62
European Economic Community, 31, 111
Exodus: from Angola and Mozambique, 107; and development strategies, 80, 81, 82, 84, 85; and labor supply, 51; of white farmers, 58, 95; of white skilled man-power, 73–74, 94, 105–106
Exports: agricultural products, 43, 55, 57, 69, 109; and balance of payments, 68–69; fishing, 60–62, 109; and household earnings, 71; mining products, 30, 31, 43, 62–64, 69, 109; new government's arrangements, 85

Farming. See Agriculture
Federal party, 36
Financing and credit: and agriculture, 57, 58, 59; industrial, 65; public, 67, 73, 81, 85; revenues, 69–71
Finland, 86
Fishing, fish-processing, 44; and development strategies, 80, 81, 110; output (table), 61; Ovambo

strike, 14; problems in, 60–62, 65, 69, 109
Fodder, 55
Food: African production, 105; from South Africa, 55, 107. *See also* Agriculture
Foreign aid, prospects of, 85, 86, 97, 110, 111
France, 1, 6, 16, 86; in Contact Group, 19, 36
Front for the Liberation of Mozambique (FRE-LIMO), 14–15
Front-line states, 19, 20, 21, 22, 24–25
Fruit, 55
Furniture factories, 65

Gaberone, Botswana, 96
Game farming, 95
General Assembly. *See* United Nations
General Mining and Finance Corporation of South Africa, 109
Geneva talks (1981), 23, 25–26, 33, 112
German Institute for Development Policy, 41
German-speaking whites, 43, 84, 94, 96, 107
Germany, 2, 17; colonists, 1–2, 3, 4. *See also* West Germany
Goats, 30
Gobabis, town, 43, 95, 96
Government: administrative structure, 74–75, 79–81; discrimination in, 72, 73; economic activities, in GDP, 67; revenues, 69–71; Turnhalle proposal, 18
Government, new administrative structure: alternative strategies, 81–87, 89; dependency-independence problems, 101–113; priorities, 94–99; South African fears about, 33–34
Great Britain, 86; African independence from, 1; in Contact Group, 19, 36; and embargo proposals, 16; and mandate status, 2, 6; and Walvis Bay, 17
Grootfontein, town, 20, 43, 45, 58
Gross domestic product (GDP): agriculture in, 55, 107; compared, per capita, 55 (table); construction, 66; fishing, 62; government, 67; and growth, 52–54, 53 (table); and income distribution, 107, 108; manufacturing, 65; mining, 54, 62, 64, 107, 109; services, 67
Gross national income, 108
Gross national product (GNP), 96
Guano, 17
Guerrilla war, South Africa-Namibia, 15–16, 18, 20–26, 38; continuation, 82; effects of, 46, 58, 59, 67, 71, 73, 88, 89; projected cease-fires, 20, 22, 25, 33, 39

Harare (Salisbury), Zimbabwe, 84
Harbors, 44
Health services, 77–79, 81, 86, 88
Herero, people: in Advisory Council, 14; cattle, 17; and land policies, 4, 9, 59; percent in population, 30; reprisals against, 1; in SWANU, 36; and SWAPO, 37, 38; and Turnhalle Conference, 16, 18
Homeland policies, 8–9
Hong Kong, 18
Hospitals, 66
Household earnings, 71
Housing, 66, 77, 86
Human rights, Carter policy, 19
Hydroelectricity, 44–45, 66

Immorality Act, 20
Imports, 45, 55, 69, 109
Income taxes, 70
Incomes, 54, 107; limited redistribution, 79–80
Independence: in Africa, 1, 7, 14, 15; and Contact Group negotiations for, 19, 20–21; and South African intransigence, 29, 99; transition to, 39–40, 71, 73–75, 88–89. *See also* Government: new Industrial Development Corporation (IDC), 108, 109
Industry, 65–67; problems in transition to independence, 80, 94, 96, 109
Inflation, 54, 71
Influx control, 35
International Court of Justice: deliberations of, 9–13, 19;

Index

injunction to Contact Group, 94; opinions of, 6–7, 8
Investors, foreign, 80
Iran, Shah of, 24
Iron ore, 62
Iscor (Iron and Steel Corporation), 109
Ivory, 17
Ivory Coast, 15

Jobs: and segregation, 35, 72
Johannesburg Consolidated Investments, 64
Jwaneng, Botswana, 96

Kalangula, Peter, 36, 38
Kaokoland, 8
Kaokoveld, 59
Kaokovelders, 30
Kapuuo, Chief Clemens, 23
Karakul, 31, 43, 55, 57, 109
Katatura, township, 43
Kaunda, President Kenneth, quoted, 104–105
Kavango: area, 43, 46, 59; people, 14, 16, 18, 30, 38
Keetmanshoop, town, 43, 45
Kenya, 86, 94
Khama, President Sir Seretse, quoted, 104
Khan, Chief Justice Mohammad Zafiulla, 13
Khomasdal, township, 43
Kunene River, 30, 32, 43, 45, 66

Labor: in agriculture, 55, 58, 107; and development strategies, 80, 81; under mandate, 3, 4; migrant, 72, 99; in mining, 64; movement of, 20, 35, 52; skilled, 73–75, 94–95, 106, 110; strike in Ovambo, 14; supply, and employment, 50–52, 71, 96
Lancaster House conference, 24
Land: acquisition and discrimination, 72–73; agricultural prices, 57; allocation, 3, 4, 57, 58, 110; arable, 30, 107; homelands policy, 8–9; reform, 74, 81, 84–85, 96, 107, 108
Langer Heinrich, mine, 64
Lead, 31, 62

League of Nations. *See* Mandate
Lesotho, 97, 101, 103, 104
Liberia, 7, 9
Libraries, municipal, 73
Literacy level, 93
Livestock farming. *See* Cattle; Karakul
Living standards, 54, 87, 88
Loans, in Namibian budget, 70, 71
Lomé Convention, 98, 111
Luanda, Angola, 15
Lüderitz, Adolph, German entrepreneur, 17
Lüderitz, poet, 17, 44
Lusaka, Zambia, 21, 102

Macao, 18
Machel, President Samora, 14; quoted, 103, 104
Maize, 55, 104
Malawi, 15, 97, 99, 101
Mandate, League of Nations, 1, 2–5; cases regarding, 6–7, 9–13; revocation, 11–12, 112; Vorster on, 35; and Walvis Bay, 17
Mandated Territory of South-West Africa, 17
Manganese, 30
Manpower. *See* Labor
Manufacturing. *See* Industry
Markets: agricultural production, 57, 58, 95–96; and balance of payments, 69; for industry, 65; shrinkage in, 97, 110; under socialism, 81
Marxists, 33, 38. *See also* Communism.
Masters and Servants Proclamation (1920), 3
Meat, 95, 109, 110
Metal works, 65
Migrant labor, 72, 99
Migration: restrictions on, 58; rural southward, 52, 60
Military service, 26, 77, 80. *See also* Defense
Mineral resources, 30–31, 62–65, 69, 95, 110
Mining, 30–31, 43, 49, 62–65; and development strategies, 80, 82; and GDP, 54, 62, 64, 107, 109; international staff for, 74; output

value, 63 (table); problems in, for new government, 85, 86, 94, 95, 110–111; and tax revenue, 69–70
Ministerial Council (South Africa), 74, 75
Ministers' Council, 18
Mixed Marriages Act, 20
Mohango, 55
Monetary policy, priorities and problems, 98
Mozambique: emigration from, 74, 107; independence moves, 14–15; rural development, 59; in SADCC, 101; and South Africa, 103, 104; in Southern African Transport and Communication Commission, 97
MPLA. *See* Popular Movement for the Liberation of Angola
Mudge, Dirk, politician: forms DTA, 20, 34, 35; lack of support, 38; ongoing leadership, 35–36
Mugabe, Prime Minister Robert, 34, 49, 97; quoted, 103
Multinational corporations, 65, 82, 84, 95, 101, 110; SWAPO policy, 108–109, 112
Municipal staffs, 73
Murray, Roger, 41
Muzorewa, Rev. Abel, 35–36, 77

Nama (Bondels) people, 4, 14, 18, 30, 38, 59
Namaland, 38
Namibia Institute (Lusaka), 41, 94, 106, 108
Namibian Constituent Assembly, proposed, 20
Namibian Independence Party, 36
Namibian National Front (NNF), 36
"Namibiazation," 84
National Assembly, 18
National Party (South Africa), 34, 38, 39, 73
Nationalization, 110–111
Native adminstrative Proclamation (1922), 3
Neto, President Agostinho, 15, 24
Newmont Mining Co., 64
Nigeria, 19
Nonproductive assets, 110
Norway, 86
Nuclear reactors, 31, 112
Nujoma, Sam, SWAPO leader, 22

Odendaal, François, report of, 8, 18
Oil, 29–30, 31, 44, 45, 62, 109
Okavango River, 30, 32, 43, 45, 66
Omaheke *sandveld*, 1
Ondangwa, town, 43
Ongwediva technical high school, 75
Orange River, 30, 32, 43, 45, 62
Oranjemund, town, 62, 64
Organization of African Unity (OAU), 102, 110
Oshakati, town, 46
Oshivello, town, 20
Ostrich feathers, 17
Otavi, town, 58
Otjihase: copper mine, 64; training center, 75
Ovambo, people: and DTA, 36; and homeland policy, 9; percent in population, 30, 43, 49; strike, 14; and SWAPO, 25, 37–38; and Turnhalle Conference, 16, 18; water in land of, 30
Ovamboland, 8, 9, 32; and agricultural modernization, 59; black technical college, 106; and DTA, 38; and independence, 83; lack of urban infrastructure, 46; representation in Advisory Council, 14; restrictive policies in, 16; and SWAPO, 38

Pass laws, 3, 20, 35
Peasant sector. *See* Subsistence farming
Penguin islands, 17, 20
Permanent Court of International Justice, 2
Permanent Mandates Commission, 3, 4, 6
Pest control services, 57
Petroleum. *See* Oil
Physical infrastructure, 43–46, 93; international development plans, 97; standards in, and future, 66–67, 89, 108
Physiography, Namibian, 30–31, 41, 43, 58, 107
Pilchards, 31, 60
Platinum, 30, 62
Poland, 111
Police: civilian, 20, 21–22; South African, 14, 22
Political parties and groups, 36
Popular Movement for the Liberation

of Angola (MPLA), 15, 16, 23, 25
Population: by age, 49 (table); by ethnic groups, 30, 42 (table); by ethnic structure (table), 45; by geography, 44 (table); geopolitical distribution, 32, 88; growth in, 50–51, 54, 58; and land redistribution, 108; and skilled staff, 84, 106; total, 41, 43, 46, 49
Portugal, 1, 14–15, 29
Postal service, 44, 97
Pragmatism: as development strategy, 86, 87, 99, 108; factors against, 101, 102, 103
Prices: diamond, 62; export, 57, 69, 71, 85, 95; increase in, and per capita GDP, 54; land, 57
Processed foods, 55
Professional services, 67
Property. *See* Land
Public debt, 71, 97–98, 111
Public sectors, 66, 74, 75, 79

Railway-artisan training center, 75
Railways, 43, 93; link to Botswana, 102; link to South Africa, 66; Namibians training for, 97; South African ownership of, 104, 109; strike in Ovambo and, 14; in Zimbabwe, 96
Rainfall, 57, 58. *See also* Drought
Rand Monetary Area, 86, 98, 109, 111
Raw materials, and industry, 65
Reagan, President Ronald, administration of, 26, 29, 33
Refugees, 20–21, 83–84
Rehoboth, town, 55
Rehoboth Affairs, Ministry of, 8
Republican party, 20
Revenues, 69–71, 70 (table); problems of new, 97
Rhodesia, independence for, 1, 24. *See also* Zimbabwe
Rio Tinto Zinc, 31, 108–109, 112
Roads, 43, 66, 93
Rössing Uranium Ltd., 30–31, 62, 64–65, 69, 107, 108, 109, 112; adult education center, 75
Ruacana Falls, 45, 66

Rural areas: development of, 58–60, 74, 79, 87–88, 89, 99, 110; status quo, 80

SADCC. *See* Southern African Development Coordination Conference
San. *See* Bushmen
Sand erosion, 58
Sardines, 31, 62
Savimbi, Jonas, guerrilla leader, 16, 32
Scandinavia, 81
Schools. *See* Education
Security, 112
Security Council. *See* United Nations
Segregation: and infrastructure, 46; reduction in Namibia, 72–73; South African, and mandate, 3–4; in Turnhalle proposed constitution, 18
Self-determination, 2, 6, 14
Self-employment, 50
Services, 67, 85; social welfare, 77–79
Sheep, 30
Shipanga, Andreas, politician, 36
Smith, Prime Minister Ian, 77
Smuts, Prime Minister Jan Christiaan, 2, 5
Social democratic development strategy, 82–87
Socialism, 81–82, 102, 105
Soil structure, 58
Solodovnikov, Ambassador Vassily, 113
Somerset West, South Africa, 95
Sorghum, 55
South Africa: African dependence on, 101, 103, 104–105; and alternative Namibian development strategies, 80–87; black education in, 75; and Contact Group negotiations, 18–26; controversy with United Nations, 5–18, 21, 22, 26, 33, 39, 40; and DTA, 34–36; importance of Namibia to, 29–33, 38–40; invasions of Angola, 15, 25; and mandate period, 1–5; Namibian economic dependence on, 46, 55, 57, 60, 62, 65, 66, 67, 71, 95–99,

101–102, 107, 108, 109–111; and national election, 36–37, 38, 88–89; and Soviet Union, 15, 29, 33–34, 112–113; and transition government, 93, 94, 95; troops in Namibia, 15, 16; and Turnhalle Conference, 16–18; and United States, 6, 15, 16, 19, 26, 29, 33, 39; white immigration to, 73–74, 105–106. See also Guerrilla war
South African Defense Force, 32, 38
South African electricity grid (ESCOM), link to, 45, 66
Southern African Development Coordination Conference (SADCC), 97, 98–99, 101–102, 110, 111–112
Southern African Transport and Communication Commission, 97
South-West Africa Broadcasting System, 44
South-West Africa National Party, 20, 73–74
South-West Africa People's Organization. See SWAPO
South-West Africa Territory Force, 26
South-West African National Union. See SWANU
Soviet Union: assistance to Angola, 32; threat of, 15, 29, 31, 33–34, 112–113
Special Committee on . . . the Granting of Independence to Colonial Countries and Peoples, 8
Steyn, Judge T. Marthinus, 20, 21, 22, 23, 24
Stock diseases, 58
Students, exodus of, 72
Subsistence farming, 43, 54, 55, 57, 58–60, 66, 79, 85, 88, 107
Swakopmund, town, 31, 43, 45, 62, 66
SWANU, 7, 36
SWAPO: as alternative to DTA, 34–36; and Contact Group negotiations, 19, 20–26, 39–40, 89; election boycotts, 9, 23; elections proposals, 37–38, 89; guerrilla war, 15, 16, 18, 20–26, 32–33, 34, 39, 73; and International Court of Justice decision (1966), 11; petitions to UN Committee, 7; support for, 8, 14, 15, 22, 26; and Walvis Bay, 18
SWAPO: as government, alternative development strategies for, 81–87; future course of action, 101, 102–113; development problems, 60, 93, 95, 97, 99; Political Program, 102, 107, 108, 110
Swaziland, 97, 101, 103
Sweden, 111
Swimming pools, 73

Tanzania, 97, 101, 103, 111
Taxes: for black labor supply, 4; diamond revenues, 62; increases in, 69–70, 86; uranium revenues, 64
Teacher-training college (white), 75
Teachers, need for, 106
Telegraph, 44
Telephones, 44
Television, 44
Temporary residents, 49
Third World, 81
Tin, 31
Tlhabanello, Mokganedi, of SWAPO, quoted, 108
Tourism, 67
Trade unions, mining, 65
Training: efforts to expand, 74, 75, 77, 86, 94–95, 106, 108; needs, 58, 78 (table)
Transnationals. See multinational corporations
Transport, 43–44, 58, 67, 88; and South Africa, 96, 97, 109
Transvaal, 38, 39
Treason, 4
Tribal elites, 108
Tsumeb, town, 43, 45, 58
Tsumeb mining complex, 14, 31, 64, 109
Tsumeb-Rundu road, 43
Tswana people, 14, 18, 30
Turkey, 3
Turnhalle Conference: constitution proposed by, 17, 18, 34–35; DTA and, 20; representation to, 16–17; Vorster and, 19–20

Underemployment, unemployment. See Employment
Union for the Total Independence of

Index

Angola (UNITA), 15, 16, 23, 32. *See also* Savimbi
United Kingdom. *See* Great Britain
United Nations: and Contact Group, 19; General Assembly actions, 6–7, 11–13, 112; International Court of Justice decisions 10–11, 12; peacekeeping force, 99, 111; possible help from, 112; possible supervision over transition, 82; Security Council actions, 12–13, 14, 15–16, 19, 21, 24, 26; and South Africa controversy, 1, 5–18, 21, 22, 26, 33, 39, 40; support for SWAPO, 14, 22, 26. *See also* Contact Group; International Court of Justice; *following entries*
UN Committee on South-West Africa, 7–8
UN Council for Namibia (South-West Africa), 12, 26, 112
UN Good Offices Committee, 6
UN High Commission for Refugees, 21, 22
UN Nationhood Program, 106
UN Security Council Resolutions: 385, 19; 435, 26, 29
UN Transition Assistance Group (UNTAG), 20, 21, 22–23, 24, 25, 26, 99, 111
United States: aid to Zimbabwe, 99, 111; in Contact Group, 19, 20; cost of UN peacekeeping force, 99; on self-determination, 2; and South Africa, 6, 15, 16, 19, 26, 29, 33, 39; State Department 29, 37; and SWAPO, 113. *See also* Carter, Jimmy; Reagan, Ronald
University graduates, 34, 105
Upington, town, 43
Uranium (oxide), 30–31, 39, 43, 62, 85; export values, 69; lessened markets for, 54, 110; output values, 64; SWAPO on sale of, 112; tax revenues, 69, 97
Urban areas: black elite in, 88; construction in, 66; housing, 77; infrastructure, 45–46; property ownership in, 84–85; and rural development, 58, 88; social development, 79, 89

Urbanization, 77, 88
Urquhart, Under Secretary General Brian, 25

Vanadium, 30, 31
Van Eck power station, 44
van Eeden Commission, 75
Vegetables, 55
Versailles, Treaty of, 2
Veterinary services, 57, 94
Viljoen, Gerrit, administrative-general, 24
von Kleist, Karsten E.B., author, 41
Vorster, Prime Minister B. Johannes: and black Africa, 15; policy changes, 19–20, 21, 23, 35

Wages, 71, 72, 80
Waldheim, Secretary General Kurt, 14
Walvis Bay, port, 44, 45, 66, 72, 87, 101; administration of, 17–18, 20; fishing industry in, 60, 62, 65; South African ownership, 21, 34, 43, 109; strategic value, 31, 62, 113
Water, 30, 45, 58, 64, 66, 108
West: future links with, 81, 86; and Namibia as bargaining chip, 33; and Namibian election negotiations, 36–37; and 1978 elections, 23; opposition to South Africa over Angola, 15; pressure by, 24, 26, 39. *See also* Contact Group, United Nations
West Germany, 19, 36, 37, 86, 111
Wheat, 55
Whites: commercial farming, 55, 57–58, 59, 85, 94, 95, 107; and DTA, 34–35; education, 5, 74, 75, 76 (table); housing, 77; income average, 54; in industry and commerce, 94, 96; land allocation, 3, 4, 8, 57, 81, 85; language groups, 43; in Namibian population, 30, 34, 49; "Namibiazation" and, 84; possible future exodus of, 75, 80, 81, 82, 84, 85, 94, 105–106, 110; present exodus of, 73–74, 79; in public and semipublic sectors, 74, 75; representation in Advisory

Council, 14; representation in Turnhalle Conference, 18, 35; resolution of Namibian problem, 40; segregation policies, 3–4, 72–73; and Soviet threat, 33; support for SWAPO, 38; suspicion of, 1–2; SWAPO policy, 107–108, 110; urban, 43, 88. *See also* Labor

Wilson, President Woodrow, 2
Windhoek (city), 14, 41, 43, 44, 45, 72, 77, 84
World Bank, 97, 105
World War I, 1–2
World War II, 1

Young, Andrew, 113

Zaire, 15, 16

Zambia, 38, 83, 86, 97, 101; and South Africa, 15, 16, 103, 104; and SWAPO, 23, 24, 36, 106
Zambian National Defence Force, 25
Zimbabwe, 97, 101, 103; compared with Namibia, 34, 49, 75, 82, 83, 84, 85, 86, 87, 89, 96, 107, 110, 112; donors' conference in, 111; elections, 25, 37; independence, 29, 33; Mudge's view, 35–36; "siege economy" in, 80; training efforts in, 77; US aid to, 99, 111; white exodus from, 74, 75, 105; white population in, 34, 49
Zimbabwe African Liberation Army (ZANLA), 83
Zimbabwe Independent Peoples' Revolutionary Army (ZIPRA), 83
Zinc, 31, 62

About the Contributors

Kate Jowell is assistant director of the Graduate School of Business Administration of the University of Cape Town.

Wolfgang H. Thomas is professor of economics at the University of the Western Cape. He is the author of *Economic Development in Namibia: Towards Acceptable Development Strategies for Independent Namibia* (Munich, 1978).

Major Nicholas H.Z. Watts (retired) has served in Western Europe, Cyprus, and Hong Kong with the Royal Green Jackets of the British Army before completing a masters degree in public administration at the John F. Kennedy School of Government at Harvard University.

Stanley Uys is London editor of the South African Associated Newspapers group.

About the Editor

Robert I. Rotberg is professor of political science and history at the Massachusetts Institute of Technology. He is the author of *Suffer the Future: Policy Choices in Southern Africa* (1980) and the coeditor, with John Barratt, of *Conflict and Compromise in South Africa* (Lexington Books, 1980).